The Vocal Coach

Maximum Vocal Performance

by Christopher Beatty

Star Song Publishing Group
A division of Jubilee Communications, Inc.
P.O. Box 150009
Nashville, Tennessee 37215

Printed in the United States of America.
First Printing, March, 1992

Library of Congress Cataloging in Publication Data
Beatty, Chris
        The Vocal Coach Maximum Performance / By Chris Beatty.—1st ed. p. cm.
ISBN 1-56233-033-0
        1. Singing—Instruction and study   I. Title.
MT820.B287 1992
783.014—dc20   92-3428
                                                                      CIP

1 2 3 4 5 6 7 8 9 — 97 96 95 94 93 92

Table of Contents

Dedication

To my parents, Samuel Fulton Beatty (1910–) and Sarah Barber Beatty (1917–1961), for putting a love and respect for the Lord and for music in my life and in my heart.

To my uncle and favorite composer, Samuel Barber (1910–1980), for inspired music that touches the soul.

Acknowledgments

My heartfelt and humble thanks to the Lord Jesus Christ for saving and redirecting my life in 1970; to my wife, partner, best friend, and coteacher Carole. That one woman could love, endure, and accomplish so much is a credit to her and to God. Also to our wonderful children, Kerri (and her husband Alan) and Scott (and his wife Karen), who have made my life so complete; to our grandchildren, Selah, Kelsey, and numbers 4 and 5 due to be "released" about the time of this book.

For my spiritual foundation to Buck and Annie Herring, for leading me to Jesus in 1970; to Pat and Shirley Boone, for sticking with me through the thick and the thin; to Pastor Jack and Anna Hayford, for being living examples of real Christianity and feeding my soul; to Jimmy and Carol Owens for their unending support and encouragement for the past 20 years; to Pastor Tracy and Connie Hansen and everyone at Community Christian Fellowship in Garden Valley for providing a place of worship, teaching, and much-needed rest.

For my technical foundation, and for sharing their hearts and knowledge, to Dr. Harvey Ringel, my college voice professor and Frederick Schauwecker, my college coach.

For hearing the Lord, our dear friends Stan and Judy Moser, Darrell and Janet Harris, and Brenda Boswell, who caught the vision of my calling.

For always being there with excellence, Matthew and Jeanie Price, David West, and the entire Star Song family.

You are all mighty tools in the hands of the Lord and a necessary part of our ministry successes.

For conceptualizing the overall look and design of our recorded and printed products we are grateful to Toni Thigpen.

For being an important part of my life, my brothers, David and Jeffrey, and my sister, Judy, and their families; Gary and Pam Boren, Dr. Larry and Carol Davis, Dr. Don and Sandy McLarey, and Ed and Zelma Lias.

For investing in the shaping of this book to Lisa Guest for her sensitive and masterful editing; to Lisa Martinson for wonderful graphics and layout.

Finally I want to thank the multiplied hundreds of students, worldwide, who have challenged and inspired me throughout the years.

In memorium: Dr. Don C. McLarey went to be with the Lord in December 1991. We are grateful for his love and investment in this ministry.

Preface

This book is for singers, speakers, pastors, teachers, athletic coaches, attorneys, salespeople, actors, aerobics instructors, radio announcers, and even mothers who find themselves vocally worn out at the end of the day. Each person in every one of these groups faces vocal performances that deserve to be delivered with maximum effect. If you belong to any of these groups, this book was written for you.

And this book was written to help you better use your voice, the most unique musical instrument ever created. What other instrument can be so dark and so bright in tone? What other instrument can produce words in any number of languages? Furthermore, the bones, muscles, and organs that comprise this instrument enable you to speak and help you breathe. They also help you worship your heavenly Father. Consider for a moment the amazing potential of your voice:

- God chose the voice to be involved in the creation of the universe. Look at Genesis 1. God speaks, and the world takes shape. God speaks again, and the moon and the stars appear. God speaks and brings animals and human beings to life. The voice—especially when the voice is God's—has incredible power to give life.
- That power to give life is available to you and me as we go about our daily lives. Do our voices clearly reflect a heart committed to the Lord and

a loving, serving spirit? Are we using our voices to encourage and build up the people around us? Are we using our voices to share the Good News of God's love and forgiveness? Are we, God's children, setting "an example in speech and conduct, in love, in faith, in purity" (1 Tim. 4:12)?

- James reminds us that "the tongue is a fire . . . a restless evil, full of deadly poison" (James 3:6, 8). The human voice can bring sorrow as well as joy. It can wound and destroy, or it can offer encouragement and hope. The power of life and death itself is indeed in the tongue, and we need to use such a mighty instrument responsibly.

- Our voice is a gift from God which, like all gifts from Him, we are called to care for wisely. (See my book *Vocal Workout* for some practical tips on caring for your voice.) And this kind of wise stewardship will result in more effective use of your voice. Besides, if there is excellence in the quality of your singing and speaking, your audience is far more likely to listen to your message, and isn't that why you're presenting it?

In light of the awesome potential of the human voice, let me encourage you to learn to use as efficiently and effectively as possible *your* voice, one of the most life-changing and, given the power and range of today's media, world-changing tools ever created.

Maximizing Your Performance

This book is the result of my love affair with the voice and a passion that may already be obvious to you. Since early childhood, I have sung, heard singing, and heard and watched singing being taught. (I still remember, as a child, hiding behind the couch in the living room listening to my mother teach voice.) I have studied and sung everything from the classics to Las Vegas show tunes to traditional and contemporary Christian music. Through the years and across this wide musical spectrum, I have been fascinated with the human voice and its ability to change people and situations.

It is, therefore, especially distressing for me to see how many Christian singers and speakers today are committing vocal suicide. Voice abuse is all around us, and it's limiting some of our greatest communicators, some of them permanently. Gifted communicators should not have shortened lives. This book is my attempt to help solve that problem.

As you work through this book, you will begin to use your voice more as God intended you to. Throughout, I offer advice on voice technique as well as spiritual insights. I've included practical tips on maximizing your vocal performance, whatever your message and whoever your audience. I've also ended each chapter with "A Brief Intermission," a set of six questions and ideas that provide you the opportunity to apply to your own life the concepts you've been reading about. I encourage you to spend time on these sections because simply reading about good ideas does not automatically put them into effect in your life. Finally, let me assure you that all that I share is based on fundamental, proven principles and methods that I have seen work for the past several decades.

Becoming Like Children

Much of what works vocally is based on lessons that young children can teach us about the voice. Think about the fact, for instance, that a baby can carry a heartfelt message over great distances for long periods of time without tiring and without suffering from laryngitis the next day. Whether an infant communicating its need for a dry diaper, a new bottle, or a hug from Mom, or a toddler entertaining us with a marathon puppet show, children can and do perform for hours—even though we sometimes wish they wouldn't!

Singers, teachers, and pastors, on the other hand, sometimes have difficulty communicating for a lengthy period of time without suffering some ill effects. What's the difference between the baby and the mature adult? The baby depends on God-given vocal techniques; adults have, however, developed their own set of rules. Guess whose way is correct? Children use their natural tone (they're not trying to impress anyone!), and they follow God's design for proper posture and correct breathing (see my *Vocal Workout* book for details). As a result, their vocal performances don't exact the physical toll that our adult performances can.

The Responsibility of Your Calling

Your adult performances are important to the kingdom. If, for instance, you are called to minister publicly in song or the spoken word, you have a great responsibility to be vocally equipped and capable. It is a mistake to assume that having a voice automatically means that you'll know how to use it correctly. Merely having arms and legs doesn't qualify you as a skilled athlete, and owning a piano doesn't make you a pianist.

You who are ministering publicly are called to understand how your voice works and how to maximize your performance. But, like all aspects of life, having this knowledge and correctly applying it are two different things. For instance, being raised in a strong, Bible-centered home is in your favor if you desire to walk with the Lord. But neither your family patterns—or family history will take the place of your personal decision to follow Jesus Christ and your commitment to act on that decision daily. Likewise, being born with musical ability and surrounded by fine music is in your favor if you want to sing. But neither natural talents nor a favorable environment will replace your willingness to be disciplined in the stewardship of your voice and the use of your voice in service to the Lord.

It's Up to You

Will this book help you maximize your vocal performance? It's entirely up to you. This book is interactive: it presents things you must do—and not just read about—if you are to improve your vocalizing and change your life. If there's no friction, there's no movement. If there's no cost, there's no accomplishment.

But I know that the cost is worth it. This book will, with your genuine effort and God's blessing, change the way you think about and use your voice. Anything that affects your communication skills affects your whole life, which means this book will affect your relationships, your livelihood, your marriage, your parenting, and even your worship. You're setting out on an exciting path toward a more fulfilling ministry. May God be with you on the journey!

Christopher Beatty, "The Vocal Coach"
Lindale, Texas

Foreword

When John the Baptist was asked who he was, he answered bluntly, simply, and revealingly: "I am a voice!" (John 1:23). *The Word* he proclaimed—Christ Himself—was the eternal, divine content; *his voice* the finite, human vehicle. The wealth of that formula is in the content—Jesus, the living Word; but the distribution of that wealth still depends on "a voice."

We are "the voice," He is the Message; we are the vocalizing, He is the Song. So it is, with the gift He's given us of *life*, we've also been made the *speakers* and *singers* of that life; each voice made to serve earth's and heaven's highest purposes.

One day, nearly 20 years ago, at a time *my* voice was wearing thin through abuse, God gave Chris Beatty's giftedness as counsel to me. It started with Chris saying, "Imagine a string tied to the top of your head. Now, pull the string straight up and let the Lord help your whole body to align and relax." That "pull" may have been the turnaround that saved *my* voice.

The intervening years have contained unique demands for a man who "voices" God's Word in five services every Sunday, and averages another three to five speaking events each week. It's to God's glory I speak His WORD. And it's to His gift through Chris' faithful ministry that I'm continually thankful; grateful for a strong voice to speak the *life* God's Word contains.

As *you* read, may your role as "a voice" be strengthened the same way . . . as you let the Holy Spirit "pull the string."

In Christ our Life,

Jack Hayford
The Church on the Way
Van Nuys, California

Chapter 1

Before the Curtain Rises

It's exciting to stand before an audience and know that you have everyone's complete attention, that they're understanding what you're saying, and that God is using you to touch hearts and lives. The joy of sharing a God-given vocal talent and a God-inspired message, the thrill of hearing the crowd's applause, and the satisfaction of a postperformance "thank you"—this kind of satisfaction is hard to beat!

And because this kind of adulation is so appealing, we who experience it need to be very aware of our motives and our message. We who are involved, one way or another, in some aspect of music ministry will be bearing fruit, either good or bad, in all that we do—and we don't need any more bad fruit in the kingdom!

These words are not to make you fearful, but rather careful and prayerful. The Lord is looking for a few good men and women to serve Him (yes, I'm borrowing that from a familiar military recruiting poster!). But effective service will come only after boot camp and only with strong leadership and ongoing training. Leave out any of those areas, and you're inviting trouble.

Your Complex Voice

As I wrote in the preface, the human voice is one of the most life-changing and world-changing tools ever created—and you and I have been blessed with that tool. And as you probably know, it's a complex instrument. It is complex in its emotional, spiritual, and physical dimensions.

- Consider that your voice reveals your soul. When you and I speak or sing, we not only share something about what is going on in our brain, but also in our heart. At times, we express our emotions directly with words. Other times, our tone of voice reveals how we're feeling. Our voice is, in part, emotion.

- Our voice also reflects our spirit. What we say to our audience, for instance, will reveal the focus of our devotion. What comes out of our mouth will ultimately reveal who or what is Lord of our life. Our words on stage, as well as our actions off-stage, will indicate God's presence or absence in our life. Our voice reveals, at least in part, the condition of our spirit.

- Most obviously, our voice is physical. Our speech and song result as numerous physical organs and, in fact, systems in our body work together. First, we inhale a breath. It then escapes through our windpipe and larynx, causing vibrations in our vocal folds. This vibrating column of air is amplified in the throat area and ultimately in the oral cavity and facial area. We then use our tongue, lips, and teeth to shape the air so that a sound can be understood. Receiving this sound is as physical as making it. Our listeners' ears respond to the moving airwaves, and their brains translate the sound into thoughts.

Since our voice has emotional, spiritual, and physical dimensions, we must keep all three and their interrelationship in mind as we work to maximize our vocal

Our voice has emotional, spiritual, and physical dimensions.

performances and our music ministry. The result will be a voice that honestly reflects what is in our heart and a heart that, ideally, reflects a vibrant relationship with the Lord and a genuine devotion to Him.

A Strong Foundation

Any music ministry calls for more than an emotional, sentimental, or even spiritual pull at your heart. It calls for a thoroughly thought-out commitment, adequate preparation, unshakable integrity, a praying support team, a regular prayer life, and constant communication with the Lord and with close friends who can hold you accountable.

Think carefully about God's call on your life. Being able to carry a tune well doesn't mean that singing needs to be your vocation. If your "calling" is based in large part on the fact that your grandmother absolutely loves your voice rather than on a clear, ongoing message from the Lord, please reconsider your direction. Know, too, that God may want your ministry to stay in your home church or local area. Does that sound limiting to you? It's not. In fact, more people are brought to the Lord and their lives dramatically changed for the better in small local churches than in all the major Christian concerts combined.

If you're considering expanding your ministry, or even "going professional," think long and hard about this question: "What is God—not your grandmother or your home church or your vocal coach or even your entire hometown—calling you to do for this season?" Not everyone spends time listening for God's direction, and the result is pain that could have been avoided. How often I've heard people say, "If only I'd known the cost to my family/my health/my spiritual life . . . " They hadn't expected a music ministry to be the spiritual battleground they experienced. They hadn't prepared themselves for the demands of the road or the demands on their voice. They hadn't rallied a support group to pray for and help them in various practical ways. They had set out to share a message they believed in, but they found that they'd somehow left God behind. Being an unprepared minister or a Lone Ranger for God can be fatal!

Again, these words are not to make you fearful, but rather careful and prayerful. A music ministry can be quite a spiritual battlefield, so be prepared! If God is calling you to serve Him in this unique and special way, respond to His call! Prepare yourself and go for it! And enjoy an exciting ministry!

How to Prepare

How do you get into the music business on a large-scale professional level, a home-church level, or anything in between? The same way a doctor gets into the medical field: by answering a calling, experiencing a genuine desire, and working very hard to prepare. Jesus Himself went through years of preparation before His public ministry began, and that's a good example for you and me. Perhaps Jesus could have been used much more dramatically by God if He had begun doing miracles at age 2. But I guess God is interested in much more than the drama of ministry—let's be sure we are, too.

And singing or public speaking, like Christianity itself, isn't learned merely by observation and hardly by osmosis. Effective vocal performance—professional or otherwise—is a participation and preparation sport and, like anything in the world of sports, it's not a good idea to be your own coach. It's better to be led by someone who has both the training and experience necessary to lead you. It's safer (you'll sustain far fewer injuries) and it's more productive (you have an objective teacher who can see what you need to work on and can help you improve in those areas).

Your training should involve the rudimentary skills of music theory and ear training. You need to be comfortable in areas like rhythm, intervals, and key signatures. When choosing a teacher, however, be careful to choose someone who is properly trained. A self-taught student of music theory can be dangerous.

And what will you gain from such study? The most important fruit of your training will be your music literacy—your real understanding of and ability to talk about your "language" of ministry. You will also be less fearful and nervous when you perform because you will know what is going on musically. You'll avoid, for instance, any gap in communication with your accompanist.

A Bit More Guidance

Before we move on to practical vocal tips for any and all kinds of performances, let me offer some spiritual tips, which many people before you have learned the hard way:

- Prepare for your ministry, whatever its scope. Then, as you recognize what God is doing in your life, you'll be ready to get right into the middle of it.
- If you volunteer for the lowest position of ministry, God can only move you up!
- You must constantly be building a foundation of spiritual discipline. It's the only foundation that won't topple.
- God's favor plus your faithfulness will be unbeatable.
- Keep your heart as well as your eyes open for ways to serve your Lord with the vocal skills He's given you. And keep in mind that His ways aren't always our ways!
- Be sure that when you perform you are sharing God's heart and not just Christian material. There's a real difference!
- If your clothing and presentation aren't believable, how can your message be? A dramatic presentation with special effects is one thing; a phony or insin-

cere heart is something quite different.
- Know what you want to leave with your audience before you begin. Work hard to leave them with God-awareness, not artist-awareness.
- You don't need to be the best in the world. You simply need to be the best you can be!
- Any time you are ministering, you are sharing the sum total of who you are. Your performance is much more than just filling a block of time with some songs and clever verbal bridges. You are called to represent yourself and the Lord as best you can. And that's what these next several chapters will help you do.

A Brief Intermission

Each chapter ends with "A Brief Intermission," a chance to apply the concepts discussed in the chapter. Why? Because simply reading about ideas is not the same as putting them into practice in your life.

- Think about a time when words have been life changing for you and a time when words have literally changed the world. In both instances, be specific about the speaker, the message, the tone, and the significance of those words.
- Explain briefly the interrelationship between the emotional, spiritual, and physical dimensions of your voice.
- Why can a music ministry be a spiritual battlefield? Learn from other people's experiences. What problems have you seen arise? And how can you avoid those problems?
- How are you currently preparing for your music ministry, whatever its scope? Who's your coach? Describe your training program.
- Which two or three tips at the end of each chapter seemed to be just for you? Write them out here and

on an index card. Then put that card in a strategic location to encourage you in your ministry.

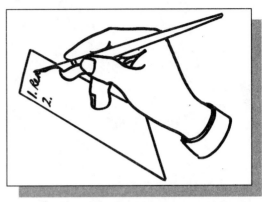

How is God calling you to use your voice for Him? Take time to listen. Outline what you think He is calling you to do now, and make it a habit to listen regularly for Him.

Write two or three tips from each chapter on a card, then put that card in a strategic location.

The ongoing instruction and inspiration available in *The Vocal Coach Newsletter* will keep you building a strong foundation. See a complete list of Vocal Coach materials at the end of this book.

Chapter 2

Learning New Music

One opportunity to perform that many people enjoy is singing in their church choir. Perhaps some of you first learned the basics of music and vocal performance before a congregation. Others of you may even direct your church's choir. Whether you are the leader or a singer, you are probably well aware of the challenges and pitfalls inherent in learning new music.

Through the years, I have come to see that the way a song is taught (or learned) has everything to do with how it is sung. In light of this fact, I offer the following guidelines for both teaching and learning a song. The first section is for group or choral music. It is followed by important tips for learning solo music. These guidelines will help the choir director, soloist, veteran choir member, shy first-timer, and, ultimately, the congregation you are leading in worship.

Learning Choral or Group Music

The following guidelines are worded specifically for the director, but those of you being directed can learn much from the perspective they offer.

1. Before your singers can become visually distracted by the music you hand out, tell them about the piece. Share about the song's message, the authorship, and any interesting historical facts you've learned. Let the singers know why you think the piece was written and why you have chosen to have them sing it.

(Simply owning the sheet music is not enough reason to sing a certain piece. If you don't have a good reason for singing it, don't sing it.)

2. Next, still before you've handed out the music, share the actual lyrics. Have the choir repeat key phrases. Allow the message to permeate the hearts of the singers before it is complicated by rhythm and melody. That way, the song will be understood at a deeper level. Since each song is a puzzle of many pieces, looking at the pieces one at a time makes the picture easier to understand and more meaningful.

3. Now hand out the music and have everyone read through the text in conversational phrases. Reading meaningful groups of words like this counteracts the choir's natural tendency to memorize words rather than learn a message. At this stage, it is more important for the choir to communicate than to mimic the director's cadence or tone.

4. Have everyone clap the rhythms, one part at a time. All clap soprano, all clap alto, all clap tenor, etc. Walking in each other's shoes like this helps give everyone a more complete understanding of the music they're making together.

5. Next, read the words in the correct rhythms. Begin by having everyone read the soprano line, then the alto, tenor, and bass. Again, by having experienced the other parts, each section will know how their part fits into the musical whole.

6. Now leave the text for a time and have every section sing each part in their comfortable octave. So that too much isn't happening at once, do this on some easy syllables such as "Nah," "Noh," "Noo," "Lah," "Loh," or "Loo." Have everyone sing one part at a time. Again, familiarizing *each* singer with *all* the parts makes for more intelligent singing and better blending.

7. This next step, one of the most valuable, will lead to an outstanding blend. Repeat Step #5 (reading the words in rhythm), but this time speak only the vowels that will be sung on each note (no consonants!). This exercise tells the articulators (lips, teeth, and tongue) what their job really is. I know this step will require some preparation on the part of the director, but it will be well worth the time and effort. Know, too, that the first time you do this it may be a bit cumbersome, but it will quickly become second nature for the group. (This part of the process is discussed in greater detail in the section on diction in Chapter 4.)

8. Now put it all together—the words, the melody, the rhythm, the parts—and sing the song as it is written.

Learning Solo Music

How should you learn a song? By singing it over and over? No! Remember that practice makes permanent and muscles have memory. If you start learning a song wrong or if you plan to learn it just by imitating another singer, you may never make that song yours.

- A good way to begin is by sitting quietly and rewriting the message of the song in your own words. Forget the meter and rhyme. Simply restate the song's message. (A thesaurus can be a real help here.) Look at this restatement of "Holy Are You, Lord." The text simply reads:

  Holy are You, Lord. Holy are You, Lord,
  Worthy to be worshiped, honored, and adored.

  Here's the rewrite:

  Divine and hallowed are You,
     my God and my King.
  Blessed, sacred, and righteous are You,
     my sovereign Savior,
  Deserving of honor, glory, and adoration.

The second verse reads:
> *Mighty are You, Lord. Mighty are You, Lord,*
> *Worthy to be worshiped, honored, and adored.*

Here's the rewrite:
> *Massively powerful and strong are You,*
> > *your Majesty,*
> *Deserving of all I am able to offer You.*

By stating in your own words what the song means to you, you have a more thorough understanding of its message, and your heart, mind, face, and body have more ways to relate to that message. Besides, the more closely connected you are to the message— the more you've made it yours—the more powerfully you will be able to communicate it to others.

- Next, tell the story of the song out loud to yourself. See if the song makes sense. Here is the story of "Holy Are You, Lord": The Lord is holy above all others. He is the only one really worthy of our worship and adoration. He is all-powerful. There is no power in this, or any other universe, that even comes close to His.

- Now try your rewritten song on someone else. Let that person ask questions about it to really test and challenge your knowledge of it. This exercise will help you determine whether you are a true communicator and not just a mimic.

Together, these steps will help you clarify in your mind the meaning and purpose of the song. Once you thoroughly understand the meaning of the song, you're ready to move on to the words that express that meaning.

Learning the Words

Words are made up of consonants and vowels. In singing, you spend most of your time on the vowels, so it's important to know what vowel you are supposed to be on at any given point. That way the articulators—your lips, tongue, and teeth—will know exactly where they are to be. Knowing your music this well won't make your singing sound mechanical or overly pronounced. In fact, knowing your words—your vowel sounds and your voiced/unvoiced consonants—makes your singing consistently clear.

- In preparing to perform my song "Holy   Are You, Lord," I begin by singing a string of vowel sounds (see Chapter 4 for details). This exercise helps me achieve real consistency and clarity of sound, especially if I concentrate on allowing the tip of my tongue to rest behind my bottom teeth for all the vowels. This technique works for every style of music from Bach to rock, and should be used by major recording artists, junior high students, and everyone in between.

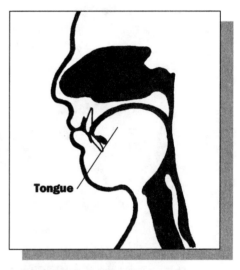

Concentrate on allowing the tip of your tongue to rest behind your bottom teeth for all vowels.

- Now it's time to memorize the words. Memory is the process of storing and retrieving information, and it actually involves a whole range of processes. When you restate and personalize the song—as we have just done in the section called "Learning the Song"—you give your mind the opportunity to better organize the material you're trying to learn. As you memorize the lyrics, use an outline or list of key words or phrases. (You can use these helps years later to quickly refresh your memory of an old song.)

This kind of mental organization leads to solid learning, and that is key to your being able to recall the words later when you perform. After all, you may face some real challenges while you're on stage. Think for a moment about the numerous distractions you'll find—everything from the child in the front row chewing gum and kicking the pew to the sound man not getting your signal to start the tape, leaving you with a few moments to ad-lib. And then there's the old "put on the wrong side of the track" surprise, which leaves you singing a duet with Twila, Sandy, Steve, or Larnelle. If you don't know your song backwards and forwards, distractions like these could mean disaster. (In the above-stated case I suggest starting over.)

At one of my concerts, the sound engineer actually left the room right when I was about to begin my first song. I had already set the stage; the audience was primed and ready. Any more talking would dilute the power of the moment. Fortunately, I'd seen the engineer leave and had immediately started considering my options. I was able to use the time by having the congregation learn a song that we would be using later in the program. I share that story to emphasize the fact that any significant amount of interference can cause you to forget your words

Think for a moment about the numerous distractions you'll find. If you don't know your song backwards and forwards, distractions like these could mean disaster.

unless they are *meaningfully etched* in your memory. Because I knew my material, I was able to take a detour and come back.

- Now read the words of the song out loud in a conversational tone that reflects appropriate emotions. If the song is a prayer, pray it. If it's a testimony, testify. And if it's a teaching, teach it. Make the lyrics real in your mind. Separate the words from the music.
- A good next step is to write out the lyrics several times, then speak the words in correct rhythm. Spend time getting comfortable with the words and rhythms together.

Next, sing the melody, but not the words. Sing "na-na-na-na" or "ma-ma-ma-ma." This gives you an opportunity to get used to the melody and the rhythms. Finally, put all the pieces together—the words, the melody, the rhythms. As you work through this process (it might best be done over several days), I know you'll be pleased with the results: a living song inside you.

A Few More Tips

Let me offer a few other ideas that you may want to share with your choir members.

- Encourage them to write standardized symbols on the music as reminders. A pair of glasses, for instance, would say to your singers, "Watch the director because it gets tricky here!" A happy face can bring renewed life, and a mouth reminds singers to keep their diction clear.
- Provide rehearsal tapes for those who want to work on an individual part.

- Make available "special help" times for those choir members willing to come early or stay late.

When you follow this process, you will be amazed by how many common rehearsal and performance problems are eliminated. And be assured that, even though these procedures seem rather tedious, this system actually saves time in the long run. This strategy has been used at every level, from professional singers to junior high groups, and it works with virtually every style of music.

The way we learn new music is an important aspect of a performance, and the method I've just described eliminates robot-like imitation and enables quality blending and unified vocal production. By dissecting the song and anticipating problems, you are almost guaranteed of more productive rehearsals and more effective singing.

A Brief Intermission

- What has been your most rewarding choir experience? What factors made it such a positive experience?

- What, for you, is the most frustrating aspect of learning a new piece of music? If you were the teacher/director, how would you eliminate this frustration?

- When has knowing some background about a song enhanced your performance? Be specific. Why did this knowledge make a difference? Explain as clearly as you can what that difference (heart, sound, etc.) was.

- Why do you think it's important for each choir member to know the other voice parts? Give three or four reasons.

- Choose a favorite praise chorus and a favorite hymn and prepare to teach them according to the method presented in this chapter. Learn the background of the song and the songwriter, chart the vowel sounds, and note any spot where your choir would need to remind themselves of something.

🦜 *Learning songs is a complex process, but while you learn new music, you can also draw closer to the Lord as you think carefully about the lyrics you are studying. This week, learn the following two songs according to the process outlined in the chapter. Be especially aware of what you're learning about the Lord and the reasons you're finding to praise Him.*

What do the words to "May His Name" mean to you? State the meaning in your own words. Then tell the story of the song.

May His Name

May His name endure forever;
May His name increase for as long as the sun shines.
Blessed be the Lord, blessed be the Lord, God of Israel.

May the earth be filled with His glory;
Let all nations call Him blessed.
Blessed be the Lord, blessed be the Lord, God of Israel.

Let us make the Lord God our refuge;
Let us here seek His will and obey it.
Blessed be the Lord, blessed be the Lord, God of Israel.

Words Psalm 72/Music Christopher Beatty. © 1982 Ariose Music (ASCAP).

Now work with the hymn "Fairest Lord Jesus." Again, state the meaning of the lyrics in your own words and then write out the story. As you do this, note how these words minister to you.

Fairest Lord Jesus

Fairest Lord Jesus, Ruler of all nature,
O Thou of God and man the Son,
Thee will I cherish, Thee will I honor,
Thou, my soul's glory, joy, and crown.

Fair are the meadows, fairer still the woodlands,
Robed in the blooming garb of spring:
Jesus is fairer, Jesus is purer,
Who makes the woeful heart to sing.

Beautiful Savior, Lord of the nations,
Son of God and Son of Man!
Glory and honor, praise, adoration,
Now and forevermore be Thine!

Spend some time praising God for those attributes featured in "May His Name" and "Fairest Lord Jesus."

Chapter 3

Mastering a Vocal Blend

In music, the term *blend* refers to the oneness of combined sounds. It's the fusion or synthesis that happens when a group of singers sing the same words and message with the same feeling, timing, spirit, and purpose. When singers are separated and independent as they sing, blend doesn't happen. When singers understand what their goal is—musically and emotionally—the potential for blend is there.

Notice that I said "potential." Blend doesn't happen automatically. What seems like effortless, natural blending is always the result of certain things being done. In the vast majority of cases, singers have meticulously worked out these vocal skills over time. In some cases, though, a good blend is simply the result of a group of sensitive vocalists singing together for a long time.

Consider the case of family groups, of brothers and sisters or parents and children who sing together. Here, good blend is often the result of common speech patterns and a special kind of commitment. When Pat and Shirley Boone's four girls sing together, for example, there is a unique and wonderful blend. The same is true of the brother and two sisters in the contemporary Christian group The 2nd Chapter of Acts. They learned similar speech patterns as they were learning to talk, and they came to understand each other as they grew up. Both these factors make it easier for them to anticipate each other's emotions and musical phrasing. This natural blend doesn't disregard good coaching and directing, but family groups do have an edge. Even if you haven't grown up with the people you're singing with, you can master the art of vocal blending.

Using Your Mind . . .

When I asked some well-known and accomplished group singers what makes their groups blend, they all referred to the same basics. First, these experienced singers said that there needs to be a shared understanding of the sound and feeling of the song. No one can ever *sing* a song more beautifully than he or she *thinks* the song. As with many areas of singing, blend is something that must begin in your mind. If you cannot think a well-blended sound, it will be almost impossible for you to sing one. A proper mental concept is the important first step toward good blend.

And that mental concept means an understanding of the feel and the message of the song. Is it happy or sad? A ballad or a dramatic testimony? Is the song to be sung with a bright or dark tone? With a breathy or a full and resonant voice? Each singer in the group needs to thoroughly think through questions like these. And until a common understanding is reached, they shouldn't sing a note.

One of the most memorable workshops Carole and I have ever done was in Wellington, New Zealand. Ninety singers from all over the city joined us, and we spent six hours together learning to stand, breathe, articulate, and sing with a naturally resonating tone. At the end of the day, we worked on a three-minute song. We talked about it, we thought about it, and then we sang it. And because we were all doing the same thing at the same time in exactly the same way, the result was breathtaking. When we finished that song, there was absolute silence in the room. Each one of us knew that we had reached the ultimate goal of unity and blend.

And Your Eyes

Besides establishing a common understanding of the song, its message, and its tone, group singers need to have a point for common eye contact—whether that be eye contact with one another (common in studio singing) or eye contact with the group's director. While such eye contact is especially important during the learning process, it is also quite valuable during performances. A point for eye contact keeps wandering minds on track and helps many sets of lips, teeth, and tongues articulate as one voice.

Eye contact with the other singers in the group is also often the quickest way to clean up shabby diction and phrasing. Simply get in small circles so you can see each others' mouths. Then, as the group sings, the members will automatically fall in step with

Get in small circles so you can see each others' mouths. As the group sings, the members will automatically fall in step with one another.

one another. In fact, the tendency is to follow those who are doing it well.

In a church choir that sings different music every week, eye contact with the conductor can never let down. In groups that perform the same music hundreds of times, the unity will often become a permanent part of the song because, as stated earlier, muscles have memory and practice makes permanent. When groups perform the same music together again and again, a conductor may not even be necessary.

Listen Carefully

The singers I talked to about blend also stressed the importance of listening to one another. They talked about hearing what the other members of the group were doing as they sang as well as what they themselves were doing. In some instances, the singers were naturally sensitive. In other cases, they had been instructed on what to listen for and how to respond to what they heard. Most of this is based on musical common sense. If you feel you're sticking out, adjust your volume and tone. (For help, see the chapter "The Tone of Your Voice" in my *Vocal Workout* book or get my *Tone I* audiotape.) You may have to experiment until you learn what works, and don't hesitate to ask for help from those with more skill than you. The skill of listening can be learned and can indeed improve your ability to blend with any group on any type of song.

But What if I'm a Soloist?

Perhaps as you've been reading along, you've been wondering whether group singing would help or hurt a soloist. I have come to the conclusion that an intelligently-used and freely resonated voice will never be harmed by singing in a group if you don't allow your voice to be abused. But be aware that, because you can't hear yourself as clearly in a group, there is a greater danger of straining your voice and over-singing even if you're a trained performer.

Of primary importance is the group's director. Is that person sensitive to each individual's voice or willing to put some voices at risk in order to get the sound he or she wants? Is he or she interested in and capable of developing and strengthening voices? If not, an inexperienced singer may very well be harmed—especially during the formative teenage years when permanent damage may result if an immature voice is abused. So, if singing with a particular group seems risky, determine the reason. Is it you or a director's unreasonable demands? If it's you, fix the problem; if it's the demands of the leader, try to bow out gracefully. But remember, under a qualified and skilled director, a soloist's voice will grow. Also, ear sensitivity and harmonic accuracy can develop especially well in a group setting.

A Note on Voices or Registers

The correct and appropriate use of chest voice and head voice are important for groups trying to blend together as well as for soloist who want a clean and full voice. Although the terms "chest voice" and "head voice" are well known, they are little understood. Sometimes these simple

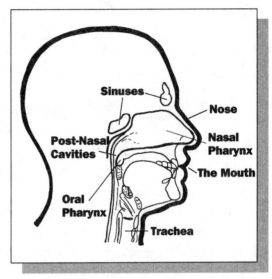

terms are even treated as special kinds of vocal tricks or techniques. Actually, "chest voice" and "head voice" merely refer to which part of your body is doing a lot of sympathetic resonating in certain ranges. After all, our bodies function somewhat like speaker cabinets with our head feeling like the tweeter, or small speaker, and our chest feeling like the woofer, or big speaker. When the head register is properly connected to and blended with the chest register, a full and rich quality results.

And we are able to produce that full sound because of the structure of the human body. Some cavities that can function as actual resonators are the mouth, laryngeal pharynx (the top of the throat), oral pharynx (the back of the mouth), nasal pharynx (the cavity behind the soft palate),

Pretend for a moment that you are a gentle, soft police siren. Using an "ah" vowel sound and with a dropped jaw and very open mouth, start in your normal speaking range and softly go up high all the way to a child's or baby's range.

post-nasal cavities (the cavities of the nose, trachea, and bronchi [air passages below the larynx]), and the sinuses in the head. This complex, God-designed acoustical cabinet called the human body is well equipped for the job of vocalizing.

Now, to feel your chest voice and your head voice in action, put one of your hands at the top of your chest, and say an affirmative, "Umhm." See how your chest vibrates? Now count to five out loud. Do you feel the vibration? If so, you're like most of us. You're in your normal speaking register or range, and that involves your chest voice.

Next, with one hand still on your chest, say, "Umhm" and count to five in a very, very high, light baby voice. You should be one and a half to two octaves higher than you normally speak. Do you feel how the vibrations in your chest disappear? You have just left the chest register.

At this point, let me mention that there is an automatic mixing of the head register and the chest register. This area of overlapping is called the passagio. For most of us, the point at which the mixing and transition will take place is around D, E, and F. As with most voice techniques, the key to a good passagio is to abandon all tension and just let it happen. Good passagio happens naturally when we let it.

To work on your passagio (alone or with a group), pretend for a moment that you are a gentle, soft police siren. Using an "ah" vowel sound and with a dropped jaw and very open mouth, start in your normal speaking range and softly go up high all the way to a child's or baby's range.

Don't worry about some slight cracking or breaking in your passagio area. Minimize it by being soft, keeping your chin down, not jutting it forward, and relaxing as much as possible. Repeat, this time coming back down to complete the cycle.

Now repeat the exercise using an "ooo" vowel sound (as in *cool*). Keep your lips rounded and slightly protruding. Massaging your throat can help keep it uninvolved during this exercise. Chapter 5, "Expanding Your Range," will give you additional exercises for smoothing out the break in your passagio.

Using Your Head Voice

The key to good vocalizing—whether with a group or in a solo performance—is remembering to move to your head voice sooner rather than later as you go up to the higher notes. Those of you who drive a manual transmission car know that it's generally damaging, or at least wasteful, to push the car to extreme RPMs before shifting up to the next gear. The same is true for your voice. Going 65 miles per hour in second gear for long periods of time will cost you. At that speed, you need to be in fourth or, if you have it, fifth gear. That's how the car—and your voice— were designed to operate. When in doubt, allow your voice to shift up just as you do in your car so that you don't overtax the instrument.

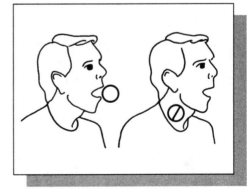

Also be aware that a more relaxed and well-blended sound will result when you bring your head voice lower, not your chest voice higher. This is especially important for tenors. Finally, when in doubt, don't shout!

The bass-baritone must learn to keep his tone focused foward in his face rather than straining in his throat.

Blending for Basses and Baritones

You may not be aware that real basses are hard to find until they're in their 40s. Most lower male voices are really baritones, and, for the sake of blending, the bass-baritone must learn to keep his tone focused forward in his face rather than straining in his throat. "Making" a bass out of a baritone leads to vocal straining and a tone that is neither pleasing or able to blend well. Bass-baritones need to begin learning to sing freely and forward in the middle and upper register. Then, and only then, can they take this forward production lower. Strive for continual facial resonance and never abandon the full range of singing when you're warming up. Maintaining your high register will help you avoid heavy, forced low tones, and you will remain balanced. And if you can't sing that low C, don't worry. Maybe God didn't intend you to.

Warning Signs and Helpful Tips

Whatever your vocal range, it's important to recognize signs that indicate you're doing something wrong whether you're singing in a group or alone. If your throat aches habitually at the end of rehearsals and your voice fails to regain its freshness within a few hours, take note. You need to take a break from singing and find out what the problem is. Then correct the problem before irreparable damage results.

Another helpful hint for singing clear, full tones and blending well is to remember to drop your jaw as you go up in range. This action helps your throat stay open and relaxed so that you avoid shrill, strident tones that will not blend with other voices.

A Group Exercise for Better Blend

Whether your group is a duo or a large choir or somewhere in between, this exercise will help clarify for members what vocal blend or unity is and is not. Divide the group into two, three, or four random groups by having members count off (for instance, "One!," "Two!," "Three!," "One!," "Two!," "Three!," etc.). Now, with the Ones standing together, the Twos together, etc., choose a note or chord that is comfortable for everyone. Have members hum that note or chord for an indefinite length of time, taking individual catch breaths whenever they need to.

Now, as the leader, instruct the different groups to change vocal quality, vowel sound, and dynamics. You might say, "Group One, change to 'ooo'. . . . Group Two, get fortissimo (very loud). . . . Group Three, get dark and strained. . . . Now all groups become soft on an 'ah.'" (Here are other possible commands: be dark and throaty, make a pinched nasal sound, sing with your chin sticking out and obviously strain your throat, sing slouched with lazy breathing, sing pianissimo or fortissimo, sing with a relaxed and pleasing tone at a moderate volume.)

As group members move in and out of different vowel sounds, tone qualities, and vocal dynamics, it will become obvious to all of them just how important it is to be doing the same thing at the same time in the same way if there is to ever be a well-blended sound.

Blending: Physically, Emotionally, and Spiritually

Blending is a skill that can greatly enhance a group's sound, and it's a skill that can be learned. And, as I've alluded to, blending happens on three levels: the physical, the emotional, and the spiritual.

- Being physically in sync—timing your consonants and vowels—is the most basic and essential aspect of blending, and this physical oneness can only be accomplished when group members watch each other. If your group has a conductor, physical blend can happen when everyone's eyes lock on that person. Without a common focus for eye contact, there will be no blend unless the group has worked on its repertoire for months and has memorized its oneness.

• An emotional blend comes when singers are literally of one mind and purpose. Those groups whose members are divided in purpose or separated by different understandings of their music will never be emotionally linked, and they'll never have a oneness of sound.

• The spiritual aspect of our lives runs even deeper than the emotional. It is at the very foundation of who we are. When combined with emotional and physical oneness, our spiritual oneness in the Lord makes possible the most complete blend of all.

As you seek better blend, remember first to establish the message and feeling of the song in your mind and heart. Also remember to maintain eye contact so that physical synchronization can happen. And, most of all, become a skilled listener. Learn to listen to others in the group so that you can learn from them. Also learn to listen to yourself so that you'll know how you're fitting in to the group's sound. Be sure, too, that you are constantly monitoring your "vitals"—your posture, your breathing, and your diction. The energy you invest in developing these skills will result in a rich and satisfying blend with other voices, a blend that will touch your listeners' hearts and give glory to God.

CHECK VITALS

✓ Posture

✓ Breathing

✓ Diction

A Brief Intermission

❧ Define *blend* in your own words and cite an example of good blend. What group have you heard that is especially good at blending?

❦ What are three important components of good blend?

❦ When have you had a "New Zealand experience"? When have you sung with a group and felt awed by the oneness of its sound? What do you think contributed to that memorable performance?

❦ Explain chest voice and head voice. How can this understanding help your singing? Your blending?

❦ Take some time this week to listen and learn. If you are currently singing in a group, pay attention to what the director does during your rehearsal time to enhance the group's blend. Whether or not you are currently in a group, listen to a group's recording. Note the characteristics of their blend. What does their singing teach you about your own participation in a group?

❦ *"Our spiritual oneness in the Lord makes possible the most complete blend of all." Keeping this statement in mind, consider the blend that the Lord makes possible in the body of believers. Read 1 Corinthians 12:4-31. What is God saying to you today through this vivid word picture of the unity of His body of believers? What, if anything, is He saying to you about your music ministry?*

Note: The *Blending I* and *Tone I* audiotapes from Star Song's Vocal Fitness Center will walk you through the dos and don'ts of good vocal blend.

Chapter 4

Perfecting Your Diction

I use the word *diction* to refer to pronunciation, enunciation, and articulation. Simply put, diction is the packaging of your words. Good diction is important to vocal performances because, whether you're speaking or singing, it promotes a more effortless and efficient use of your voice and more effective communication.

Pronunciation, Enunciation & Articulation

DICTION

Diction is the packaging of your words.

While you're in the process of improving your diction, be patient. No one is expecting you to suddenly change dozens of habits that took years to develop. That process will take time, but you can begin this very day. The principles I'll present apply to speaking as well as singing, to music ranging from classical to pop, and, with little exception, to solo as well as group singing.

God's Design

If I were speaking this chapter to you out loud and mumbling the whole time, you'd find it a lot more work to keep up with what I was saying. You'd also find yourself mentally and possibly even physically exhausted from the strain of trying to figure out what I was saying. If, however, I had worked on my diction, you would probably find it easier to listen to me, and I would find it easier to communicate to you the ideas I wanted to share.

When we work within the physical design that God developed, our speech is more effective. When we alter that design (physically or chemically), the entire system fails. For instance, people under the influence of drugs and alcohol don't communicate clearly because the chemicals they have ingested interfere with God's design for mental and physical coordination and so affect their speech. The key to good diction is to work within God's design—don't abuse it!

Diction and Your Message

Have you ever listened to someone who was working so hard on correct diction that that person's face seemed to move from one contorted expression to another? You were probably so distracted that you didn't even hear what the person was saying! Or what about the "ventriloquist syndrome" that attacks some teenagers when they are asked a question? You know they are talking, but they are expressionless. They hardly move their mouth, and their face is definitely in neutral.

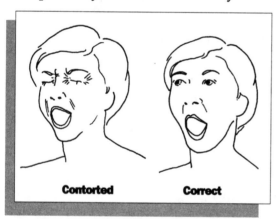

Contorted   **Correct**

It's important, that your diction match your message so that your listener doesn't have to work hard to really hear what you're saying.

Both these extremes—overarticulating and underarticulating—can be very distracting. Both can turn your listener's attention away from what you're saying to a fascination with your amazing facial expressions or your seemingly miraculous production of sound without movement. It's important, therefore, that your diction match your message so your listener doesn't have to work hard to really hear what you're saying.

Let me also caution you to be sure to pronounce your words correctly. Whether referring to ancient biblical figures or current world leaders, names do have correct pronunciations, and mispronouncing names (or any other words) can distract and even destroy your message. Prepare and practice in advance to be sure that your vocal performance won't be marred by mistakes. Errors in pronunciation are easy to avoid. It just takes a little preliminary work and prior planning.

How Did I Get This Way?

Our diction—including our accent, vocabulary, and delivery—is the result of imitation and alteration. The reason people can often tell where you're from is that you, your family, and your neighbors all speak the same way. You have quite possibly imitated not only the content but also the delivery of the people living in your hometown.

Take, for example, a salesperson from East Texas and one from New York City. Forget the obvious differences in accent and consider the intensity of the delivery. New Yorkers live in a far more stressful and crowded setting, and this is reflected in their speech, manners, and mannerisms. They talk faster, louder, and with greater expression than their average East Texas counterpart. The East Texan lives in a more rural, relaxed, and slower-paced setting. You are likely to end up talking about the weather, your family, and the local high-school football team before the sales call is over. If someone in a big city asked about your family, you'd probably dial 911 and run! (Now if you are from one of these areas and I have offended you, forgive me. My descriptions aren't true for all the folks in those areas, but I can testify that it's pretty close to all!)

So how did you come to speak the way you do? The same way the New Yorker, the East Texan, and I did. We all learn by imitation. But as adults we can, by being aware of our diction and delivery, work through certain exercises, and change the way we present our words.

Taking Inventory

As you know, words are made up of vowels and consonants. When we speak, we spend proportionately more time on consonant sounds. When we sing, we spend more time on vowels: the vowel sounds are elongated and the pronunciation of the consonants is often delayed. The vowels carry the notes and tone and make a song singable. This basic pattern, however, can be affected by the speech pattern unique to each one of us.

And analyzing your personal speech pattern is the first step in learning about diction. Your normal, everyday speech patterns affect your singing, so it's important to know what your speech patterns are and how they may be influencing your singing. The following questions will help you begin to identify some of your speech patterns:

- Do you clearly pronounce your l's? Do you say, "He 'oize' does that" or "He always does that"? In the supermarket the other day, I heard a page for a Mr. Weeyums. I knew the person being paged was Mr. Williams, and I also knew that if I slowly pronounced both versions for the person doing the paging, that person would change the pronunciation. "Mr. Weeyums" would become "Mr. Williams." Fortunately for my wife and the other shoppers, though, I didn't offer my minilesson in diction. But the supermarket story helps make an important point: as you become more "diction aware," you'll begin to automatically change the way you speak. This change will, in turn, enhance your singing.

- Do you add extra syllables to certain words? In the well-known Christmas opera *Amahl and the Night Visitors* by Gian Carlo Menotti, Amahl's mother sings, "Are you sure, sure, sure?" and Amahl responds, "I'm sure, Mother." But what if the singers added a regional ending to that word? Imagine them singing, "Ah you shoe-ah, shoe-ah, shoe-ah? I'm shoe-ah, Muthuh." Being aware of your tendency to add extra syllables to words can help you clean up your singing.

- Do you make single-syllable words into two-syllable words? *Well* is a one-syllable word, but some people say, "why-ell." We may laugh if that doesn't happen to reflect our own regional accent, but it's important to remember that an enormous variety of accents exist in the United States. Since there is no national standard of speech for English, learning to neutralize and purify our vowels and consonants will help us be more easily understood by a greater number of people.

Let me interject a personal note here. When Carole and I moved from Southern California to East Texas, our son Scott was still living at home with us. He opted to transfer to a local university in Texas for his last two years of college. His first semester, however, was nearly traumatic since his California ears had great difficulty interpreting East Texas speech patterns. By the second semester, though, he had adapted and all was well.

The preceding questions and thoughts can begin to sensitize you to speech patterns, your own and those of the people you hear all around you. An even more effective tool for analyzing your own speech patterns, however, is a tape recorder. Even a short recording of your speaking and singing can reveal much. It may help you recognize that the speech patterns you grew up with—and therefore assumed were correct—are not accepted everywhere. After all, "correct" and "easily understood" are two different things. Record yourself reading from the Bible, a newspaper, or a magazine. Then record the passage a second time, pronouncing the words as a network newscaster might. Do you hear the difference? Having listened to your tape, you may now have an even greater awareness of your own unique speech patterns.

The Singing–Speaking Connection

Enough about what you're doing now. Let's move on to what we can do to become more effective in our speech. I want to begin by introducing you to a vocal-production paradox: speech that is well spoken is half sung, and well-sung songs generally have a speechlike element. In other words, speech is best when there is a degree of flow and connectedness, and good singing is believably conversational. After all, singing is really sustained speech.

Consequently, studying speech to sing well and studying singing to speak well makes sense. Successful singers and speakers have done it for years. (It's like football players who study ballet. They do so for agility and balance, not because they want to perform with a dance company.) Since singing and speaking are produced by the same mechanism, they are related at every level. The greatest difference other than the music is simply the elongation of the vowel and the placement of the consonant in singing.

Studying speech to sing well and studying singing to speak well makes sense. It's like football players who study ballet.

Diction Exercises: Vowel Sounds

- It's important to train your ears to be "vowel aware." One way to do that is to sing a song in a very unusual way, a way that will train your mind and ear to analyze the vowel sounds. You do this by leaving out the consonants.

  As you sing the following phrases, imagine yourself singing only the vowels. If you're not a musician or don't have a piano handy, just speak the song in a very s-u-s-t-a-i-n-e-d manner.

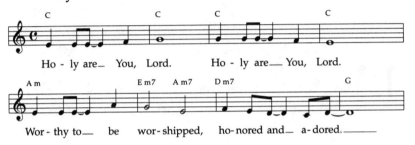

Ho - ly are— You, Lord. Ho - ly are— You, Lord.

Wor - thy to— be wor - shipped, ho-nored and— a-dored.———

©1982 Ariose Music (ASCAP)

Now, taking a phrase at a time, analyze the vowels. The word *holy* has two syllables: ho-ly. The vowel sound for the first syllable is "oh," and the sustained vowel sound for the second syllable is "ee." With the tip of your tongue resting behind your bottom teeth, say, "He." Feel where your tongue is. Leave the tip of your tongue in this home position for all vowels. With the tip of your tongue still in position behind your bottom teeth, say, "Oh Ee." Now say, "Ho-ly."

The word *are* has a single vowel sound. It is "ah" as in *father*. Say, "Ah." Now, with the tip of your tongue resting behind your bottom teeth, say, "Oh Ee Ah." Now say, "Oh Ee Ah—Ho-ly are." The tip of your tongue goes up behind your top teeth for the *l* in *holy*, but the rest of the time (except for the *r*) it stays in home position behind your bottom teeth. For the *r*, slightly round your lips. Keep the *r* sound clear and very short.

Now for the word *you*. The sustained vowel sound is "oo" as in *moon*. The sounds that you sustain when you sing, "Ho-ly are You" are "Oh Ee Ah Oo." Sing that: "Oh Ee Ah Oo." Now sing it (or speak in a sustained manner) first with just the vowel sounds and then with full words: "Oh Ee Ah Oo, Ho-ly are You. Oh Ee Ah Oo, Ho-ly are You." Your articulators and your brain are teaming up in a new way.

The word *Lord* also has only one principal vowel sound. Say the word slowly: "L-o-r-d." The vowel sound is "oh." With the tip of your tongue resting behind your bottom teeth, say, "Oh Ee Ah Oo Oh." This time sing (or speak in a sustained manner) the vowels and then the full words: "Oh Ee Ah Oo Oh. Ho-ly are You, Lord." When you're singing the full words, concentrate on producing pure, sustained vowel sounds and using the home position for the tip of your tongue. The *rd* of *Lord* is pronounced clearly but briefly.

- Next, think about vowels in your everyday speech. Say, "Hello." Now say, "Eh Oh." Say, "Hello, Eh Oh," but don't start the vowels "eh oh" with a glottal stop. (Feel the catch in your throat when you say the *a* in *after*? That catch is a glottal stop.) A glottal stop can be really hard on your vocal cords. Instead, use a very slight, silent "hhh" before you say, "Eh Oh."

- Read the following words and phrases. Focus on pronouncing the neutralized vowels that a network TV or radio announcer would use:

  This is fun. Ih Ih Uh.

  How are you? Ah-Oo Ah Oo?

I'm fine. Ah-Ee Ah-Ee.
What time is it? Uh Ah-Ee Ih Ih?
Are you happy? Ah Oo A (as in *cat*) Ee?
Let's go on. Eh Oh Ah.

- Say the following single words and their sustaining vowel sounds. Be aware of your tongue position (the tip resting behind your bottom teeth) and try to anticipate the vowel sounds:

Cat	Dog	Fish
Window	Book	Tree
Go	Scott	Kerri
Karen	Alan	

Remember that part of the key to changing is becoming an alert listener: what vowel sounds are you hearing yourself and other people make? As you become more and more aware of vowels in your own daily speech and that of other people, your singing and public speaking diction should become clearer.

Diction Exercises: Consonant Sounds

Consonants can be divided into two groups: the voiced and the unvoiced or voiceless. A voiced consonant can actually vibrate; the unvoiced cannot. There are nine pairs of these voiced and unvoiced consonants in the English language. We'll identify some of them now.

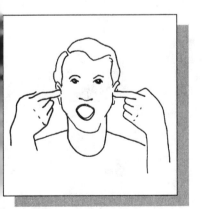

Say "b" & "p." Say it twice. Now put your fingers in your ears and say it twice again. Which vibrates?

- B and P — Say *b* as in *boy*. Say it twice. Now put your fingers in your ears and say it twice again. Feel the vibration? This *b* is a voiced consonant. You can feel it vibrate.

Now say the consonant *p* as in *pay*. Say it twice. Plug your ears and say it twice. This is an unvoiced (or voiceless) consonant, so there is no vibration.

Now wrap your hand around the front of your throat and alternate between the voiced *b* of *boy* and the voiceless *p* of *pay*. The *b* and the *p* are formed in exactly the same way. The only difference is that one vibrates and the other does not. You should clearly feel the difference between the vibrating of the voiced *b* and the lack of vibration of the unvoiced *p*.

- D and T—Now say *d* as in *dog* and *t* as in *take*. Repeat the sounds a few times. Plug your ears and say the sounds twice. Now with one hand on your throat, say, "D T D T." Do you feel the difference? The *d* vibrates; it's a voiced consonant. The unvoiced *t* does not make your throat area vibrate. Both sounds are formed the same way.

- G and K — Say the sounds for *g* and *k* as in *girl* and *kiss*. Which one is voiced and has vibration? Say the sounds once again, this time with your fingers in your ears. The *g* is voiced; it vibrates.

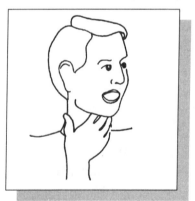

Wrap your hand around the front of your throat and alternate between *b* of *boy* and *p* of *play*. Feel the difference?

- Now compare two words. The first one begins and ends with voiced consonants. Slowly say, "Dig." Now plug your ears, say the word a couple times, and feel the vibration throughout the word.

Compare that to the word *take*, which begins and ends with unvoiced consonants. Slowly say, "T-a-k-e." Repeat it. Do you notice that the only vibration comes with the vowel? Say, "Take" with your fingers in your ears and then with a hand on your throat. The *t* and the *k* have breath, but no vibration.

Now say the two words together: "Dig. Take. Dig. Take." Plug your ears and repeat the words. Say them again, this time with a hand on your throat. Notice the vibration and lack of vibration.

- V and F—Say the consonant sounds *v* and *f*. Repeat them. Now say, "Very." Say it again. The sound is voiced; you can feel the *v* vibrate. Even though the *f* sound is formed the same way, it doesn't vibrate. Say, " Fine." Do you feel the breath? Say it again— "Fine." Now say, "Very. Fine." Repeat it. You know the routine. Now plug your ears and say, "Very. Fine." Do you hear the difference? Do it again with a hand on your throat: "Very. Fine."

- Th—The *th* sound can be voiced or unvoiced. Say, "This." Plug your ears and say it again. The *th* vibrates, doesn't it? So it must be voiced. But now say, "Thought." Say it slowly: "T-h-o-u-g-h-t." You feel breath, but no vibration on the *th*. Now say, "This thought." Again, "This thought." Notice the voiced and the unvoiced consonant sounds.

- S and Z—Speak this phrase slowly: "He wonders how to say it." The *s* of *wonders* is voiced; it vibrates. Say, "Wonders" slowly and feel it vibrate. Now say, "Say." The *s* in *say* is formed the same way the *z* sound of *wonders* is, but one is voiced and one is not. Now say, "This is." Which *s* is voiced? Which is unvoiced?

When you speak and sing, you should clearly understand what vowel sound you are sustaining and whether the consonants are voiced or unvoiced. This awareness will help you communicate more consistently and more clearly.

Does this analysis of vowels and consonants seem excessive? It's not. Just as years of studying addition and subtraction let you immediately know if you get the correct change from the cashier, this study will help you instinctively speak more clearly.

The Problematic R

When we move from speaking to singing, we suddenly recognize that the letter *r* is awkward and often hard to deal with. Elongating the *r* can be very offensive in almost every style of music except, perhaps, country ("Mah hahrrrrt's filled with glohrrrrray").

The traditional classical approach in singing is to eliminate the *r* before a consonant. I find that a bit disturbing because, in most situations, you end up with words that don't exist in my vocabulary. Is it a "wintuh moning" or a "winter morning"? Do you see the "stahz in summuh" or "stars in summer"? Does the "Lod have muhcy" or does the "Lord have mercy"? You decide.

Since most of us are singing English in America, we do need to sing the *r*. Let it be there, but don't let it be ugly or overdrawn. I find the most practical solution to be either making the *r* fairly short or making sure your lips stay open, rounded, and not too protruded. Say these words: "Summerrrr. Summuh. Summer." Now say them again with protruding and overly rounded lips. Which sound do you prefer?

The Diphthong

Another challenge for singers and speakers is the diphthong, the occurrence of two vowels in a single syllable. When you confront a diphthong, be sure to sustain the first vowel sound for most of the syllable; you'll only close with the second sound.

Imagine singing the word *how* with the vowel sounds "Ah-OO." Sustain the first vowel and close the syllable with the second. Say, "Hah-----oo." That's correct. Now say, "Hah-OOOOOOOOO." That's awful. There are exceptions to this rule in some musical styles, but first learn the norm.

The Power of Clear Speech

Have you ever thought about how much of your day involves speaking or listening to someone else speak? And have you ever noticed that those people who speak the most clearly are often the ones whom others follow no matter what they're saying? Consider any of a number of figures from world history or even today's newspapers. Despite murderous ideas, certain leaders have had followers willing to kill for them. The ability to speak, motivate, and persuade can end the lives of thousands, change the lives of millions more, and greatly alter the course of world history. We can't underestimate the impact that effective speech—both good and evil—has on our world. In light of the tremendous potential of speech, it is my prayer that your speech and song will be much-needed light in this world.

Putting It All Together

Let's finish this chapter by singing once again "Holy Are You, Lord." First sing only the vowels; then sing the full words.

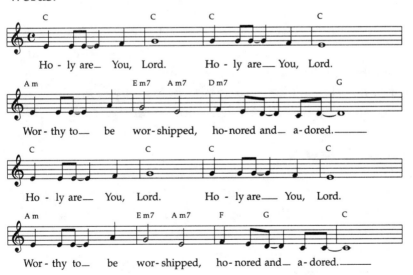

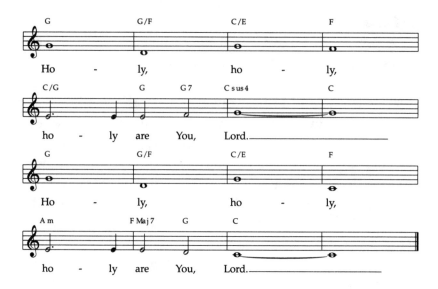

As you sing, remember your vitals. Proper posture and correct breathing underlie all effective speech and singing. Maintain a balanced head position and keep your chin down. Get in the habit of using the "home position" for the tip of your tongue. (It's easier on your voice, gives you more consistency, and helps you blend with a group.) And of course pay attention to your pure vowel sounds and your voiced and unvoiced consonants.

Is this all there is to diction? No. It's just scratching the surface. It is, however, a good first step toward becoming more aware of what you are doing now in speech and song. Besides, it's easy to apply these daily exercises, and they will tend to clear up your singing and speaking.

A Brief Intermission

- Define *diction* in your own words.
- Review the section titled "Taking Inventory." What patterns are characteristic of your speech? What habits have you developed through the years? Do you mumble or overpronounce your words? Do you drop final consonants, mispronounce cer-tain words, or pronounce words inconsistently? Do you speak with

a heavy or annoying accent or in a dialect that not everyone understands?

List two or three qualities of your speech and note one that you would like to begin to change. Being conscious of these characteristics is an important first step.

❦ Singing and speaking: How are vowels and consonants treated differently in speech and in song? Explain the somewhat paradoxical connection between singing and speaking.

❦ Little things can make a big difference. Define the following little things that can make a big difference in your vocalizing:

- What is the home position for the tongue? And why is that position important to singing?
- What is a glottal stop? What is a good alternative to a glottal stop?
- Explain the difference between voiced and unvoiced consonants and give three examples.
- What are two ways of dealing with the problematic *r*?
- What is a diphthong? How should a diphthong be sung?

❦ Write five sentences on any subject you're interested in. As you write, pay attention to voiced and unvoiced consonants and begin to hear the difference. Also, hear in your mind the pure vowel sounds that a skilled speaker or singer would produce. Then read the sentences aloud to someone who can help you determine if and when your speech patterns are influencing your diction.

❦ *Clear and effective speech can and does change lives and alter the course of history. Choose a passage from the Bible that has significantly influenced your life and prepare a reading of it. Be sure to know how to pronounce every word in neutralized American English. Be aware of your facial expressions. Concentrate on the vowel sounds and voiced/unvoiced consonants. Let these elements of your reading enhance your presentation. Effective reading can help people hear afresh even a very familiar passage from Scripture. Practice with a tape recorder. When you're ready, share the passage with an audience of one or ten or more, preferably others who have also prepared a passage. Close that time by thanking God for His living and life-changing Word!*

Note: To hear and experience these diction principles, I strongly recommend *Diction I,* an audio teaching tape from Star Song's Vocal Fitness Center.

Chapter 5

Expanding Your Range

Have you ever listened to a gifted soprano and wished you could hit the high notes that she does? Or have you heard a baritone hit a low note and wondered how he does it? At one time or another, I think we all wish our vocal range were wider than it is. This chapter will help you realize that your potential range is probably greater than you think. Then it will put you on the road to achieving that wider range you wish you had.

The Range of Your Voice

First, let me define *vocal range* as those notes which, given your physical mechanism and your normal technique, you are able to sing with relative freedom. Notes within that range do not damage either your voice or your listeners' ears.

Expanding this range will open up more styles of music to you and increase your repertoire. Expanding your range will also make you a more flexible and valuable singer when you sing with choirs or other groups. While your goal may be to expand your performance range as much as possible, my goal is to help you increase that range safely—and that means slowly. Expanding your vocal range is like building body strength. It can't be done with magic, drugs, or overnight. By gradually developing a greater range, you will be less likely to strain your voice. Consequently, your voice will be healthier and last longer.

Determining Your Current Range

A good first step toward expanding your vocal range is to determine where you are right now. With a piano, guitar, pitch pipe, or some other appropriate instrument, sing some simple scales. Your goal is to find the most comfortable top and bottom of your comfortable range.

As you determine your present range, remember that there is an important difference between singing a note and hitting a note. When you sing a note, you are in control, and your face and neck are quite relaxed. When you hit a note, though, you are probably pushing beyond what your voice is able to do well—at least at this time—and your throat muscles are hardly relaxed. If someone can take your pulse from 50 feet just by looking at the bulging veins in your neck, you are hitting notes, not singing them. Or if the only way you can "sing" some notes is by putting your head in a certain and probably unnatural position, you are straining, not singing. You are limiting what your voice can do by stifling instead of stimulating the natural instrument.

Indicate your comfortable top and bottom notes here:

The Tessitura of a Song

Once you determine your vocal range, you will be able to know if a song fits within that range. What are the highest and lowest notes in a given song? Those two extremes indicate the song's range.

Sometimes when you ask about the range of a song, though, what you really want to know is the song's tessitura. Where do most of the notes in your part lie?

Knowing the average note of the song—the tessitura—can be even more helpful than knowing its range because most of us are comfortable popping up to a few high notes during a song, but we wouldn't be comfortable staying there all day!

The following example demonstrates how two melodies can have the same range but different tessituras. In the first line, the notes range from C to E, a range of an octave plus a third. The tessitura, or average note, is quite low, closer to the bottom than the top of the range. It's about an E, the fourth note in the phrase.

In the second line, the range is the same (C to E), but the tessitura, or average note, is quite high, making this line a totally different singing experience. It centers around B, the twelfth note in the phrase.

Conclusion: you can't tell everything about a song by its range.

A Singer's Comfortable Range

It's important for choir directors—and for choir members themselves—to recognize the tessitura, or comfortable range, of their own and other members' voices. The difference between a high tenor and a low tenor, for instance, may not be the highest or lowest notes they can sing. It may be where they are most comfortable singing for a long period of time—their average comfortable notes or, in a sense, their tessitura. The same is true for sopranos, altos, basses, and baritones, and that fact should help explain why you may seem to tire on certain songs while other people in your same voice classification don't. The problem may not be the range of the song, but its tessitura or yours. That particular song may simply match the range of the other singers and not quite fit with yours. That doesn't mean that you refuse to sing your part, but it may mean that you sing it differently or more carefully.

A Word about Voice Classifications

As you discover your full range and even expand that range, you may need to change your voice classification. Remember that every vocalist has a comfortable median range, and let me offer you this important word of caution as you work to increase yours. Vocal longevity and vocal comfort are directly related. In other words, if you want your voice to last, don't push it too hard to be what it's not!

Your vocal range should be limited only by the size and shape of your vocal mechanism. If your vocal folds or vocal cords are thick and long when they're relaxed, you are probably either a bass or a contralto. On the other hand, if your cords are shorter and thinner, you are either a child, a tenor, or a soprano. And there are many steps between those two extremes.

But let me make an important point here. God did not create coloraturas, sopranos, mezzos, altos, contraltos, tenors, baritones, bass-baritones, and basses. He created people. We human beings have categorized voices to make identification easier for choral purposes, but many times this labelling system is not very accurate, generally at the expense of the singer. In many choirs, people are singing the wrong parts either because no one knows better or because there is a need for more singers of this or that part.

Choir directors, let me say to you that violins simply can't play bass notes and cellos don't sound good playing high violin parts. Why? Because they aren't built to create those sounds. Likewise, voices are "built" to create sounds within a certain range and shouldn't be forced to create other sounds. So it's important for those in charge to keep voices where they should be. Change the arrangement or even the repertoire if necessary, but don't ruin voices just to make a certain

Choir directors shouldn't confuse gender with voice parts. Some men are wonderful high tenors who can boost the alto parts.

song work in one particular way. It's not worth it and it's simply not right. All too often I encounter people whose voices have been pushed, strained, and almost ruined by choir directors who are more concerned about arrangements than people. Don't be one of those!

One more note on vocal classifications. I want to caution singers and choir directors alike: don't confuse gender with voice parts. Some of the best tenors are women because that range is where their voices lie, and some men are wonderful high tenors who can boost the alto parts better than some of the women in the group. It's important for those of us involved in vocal performance to start thinking "God made" rather than "man defined."

Age and Range

Your age also has something to do with your vocal range. Preteens, of course, are not physically developed in the larynx, and boys especially don't yet have much of a lower range. In their early teenage years, both boys and girls are still very much developing and should not push their voices beyond what the instrument can easily do. These young singers should, however, be working to perfect their posture, breathing, and basic tone.

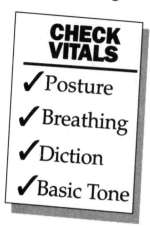

CHECK VITALS

✓ Posture

✓ Breathing

✓ Diction

✓ Basic Tone

At the other end of the spectrum are singers well into their 60s and 70s. Here, too, there are some age limitations, but not many. Most vocal limitations that occur in our later years are due to not maintaining good posture and proper breathing and not paying attention to basic voice technique. But let me assure you that it's never too late to correct those things. Rediscovering posture and breathing as God designed them and learning good voice technique can mean discovering a new strength and range in your voice and a healthier you. And working with our *Breathing, Warm-up,* and *Daily Workout* audiotapes can help restore accuracy and agility to any voice.

Singing Clearly Throughout Your Range

Fundamental to expanding your range is understanding certain areas of your existing range—specifically, your head voice, chest voice, and passàgio—which I mentioned in Chapter 3. Remember the speaker cabinet?

- As you sing higher, you reach a point where areas in your head are just the right size to enhance those higher frequencies. Here you are singing in your *head voice.*
- When you are singing in a lower register, you are in your *chest voice.*
- The *passagio* is where these two voices meet, and it is characterized by a blend of the two registers. As I said earlier, the area where the transition will take place for most of us is around D, E, and F. (The exercises in Chapter 3 will better illustrate these terms

by helping you recognize which part of your body is doing most of the resonating when you are producing certain sounds.)

Whichever register you are singing in, you will always be striving for clear vocal tone. Creation of that tone begins when nerve impulses from your brain tell your body that a sound should be produced and just what pitch and emotion that sound is to have. Understanding how your voice works—where it starts, what creates the sound, how the sound waves vibrate in your built-in woofer and tweeter, and how to produce clear vowel sounds—will help your voice work better. Take the time and make the effort necessary to develop this understanding.

Increasing Your Range
Now let's get to work with the following exercise:

Fall foward at the waist and, hanging limp, slowly stand back up, a vertebra at a time.

- With your knees slightly bent, begin by falling forward at the waist and hanging limp like a rag doll. Slowly stand back up, a vertebra at a time, feeling your lower vertebrae straighten up first and then continuing up your spine until the top of your head is as far away from the floor as possible. With your shoulders relaxed and your head aligned with your tailbone, start by speak/singing (very sustained speech on no particular note) these patterns: "Zee ah zee ah zee. Flah flah. Ng ee ay ah." (The *ng* is the sound at the end of the word *sing*.)
- Move from a comfortable and low speaking register to a floating high and light note. Keep your jaw dropped

open wide on the "ah" vowel sound, and make sure
the tip of your tongue is resting behind your bottom
teeth (where it is when you say the vowel sound "ee")
on all vowels. Don't worry if there's a slight break,
crack, or jump in your voice as you move through the
passagio area.

The Expressionless Statue Siren Exercise

- Now, standing very tall with the top of your head as
far from the floor as possible, imagine that you are a
motionless statue that has been placed against a wall.
Your chin is down, you are looking straight ahead,
and your face is expressionless. The only noticeable
movement in your body is the breathing action at
your waist.
- Now take in a full low breath, letting your waist—
the front, sides, and back—expand fully. Gently drop
your jaw and, in a normal speaking voice, say, "Yah."
Repeat. This time, with absolutely no move-ment in
your throat, say, "Yah" again and let it slide up in
pitch, like a siren, from your normal speaking voice
to as high as you can while staying reasonably relaxed in your throat. Keep the sound light and airy.
Allow your jaw to drop farther open the higher you
go and then recover gradually as you come back
down. Don't lock or tighten your jaw or throat
muscles. Just let the sound happen. There's a good
chance that your voice may break or crack slightly
in the passagio. That's fine. Just be soft and gentle in
that range until your voice grows stronger over the
next few weeks. Your laryngeal muscles will learn
the ropes if you allow them to.
- As you do this exercise again, keep in mind the
following: as the pitch gets higher and then lower,
there are no parallel movements in your head or
throat. In fact, if you were in a soundproof room,

someone observing you through a window should not be able to tell if you are singing high notes or low notes.

- After doing this exercise a few times, jot down the low and high notes you can hit effortlessly. Next to that, put down the comfortable top and bottom notes (your current range) that you wrote earlier in the chapter. Somewhere between those two high notes and those two low notes lie the top and bottom notes of your new range.

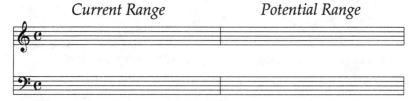

Current Range   *Potential Range*

Rules to Practice By

Before we move on to a few more exercises, I want to remind you of the four rules for your warm-ups, your practice sessions, your voice lessons, and your performances—rules for whenever you sing!

1. Constantly be monitoring your posture. Keep your head as far away from the floor as possible with your shoulders and your chin comfortably down. When your head is not in that proper position, your voice can sound strained. When you're holding it in its natural position, your head enables you to produce a relaxed sound and consistent tone.

2. Breathe low and full, expanding your abdomen, sides, and back and not moving your chest and ribs.

3. Help keep your throat relaxed by gently massaging it while you sing—except when you're per-forming! If you feel your throat get tight and strained during these exercises, stop! Check the position of your head and chin to be sure that you're not putting

undue stress on your throat.
Also, allow your vocal mechanism to take you naturally into
your head register.

4. Whenever you're singing a
vowel, allow the tip of your
tongue to rest behind your bottom teeth. This position reminds
your tongue not to pull back into
your throat and encourages clear
voice quality and pronunciation.

Correct posture, proper breathing,
a relaxed throat, and a forward tongue
position—four points which I can't

Keep your throat relaxed by gently massaging it while you sing.

emphasize enough—are key to maximizing your vocal performance even when you're just practicing. And remember: practice makes permanent!

Back to Work

- On this exercise, stay very conversational and "talky"
  while you move through your range from the lowest to the highest extremes. On the lower notes, your
  voice will sound like normal speech; on the higher
  notes, you will sound light and almost childlike. The
  sound can, however, be quite connected, and that is
  the goal of this exercise.

  Remember to keep your posture balanced and your
  chin comfortably down as you lightly speak, "Mah
  mah mah mah." Now, as you move from your speaking range well into the high extremes of "Baby-voice-
  land," keep the sound light. And keep that throat
  relaxed at all times. It should never tighten, nor
  should you allow your chin to stick out and extend
  beyond the point of good balance. Such maneuvers
  will only hinder your vocal production. It is better to
  stay relaxed even if your voice does crack or break

some. That will be smoothed over in time if you allow it. Also remember that lightly massaging your throat while you exercise will help keep it relaxed.

- Next, replace the previous syllables with something that you can do anytime you're in an uncrowded area, and that's humming. Using the same random notes and making up a melody as you go, this time hum lightly instead of using "mah," "bah," or "pah." You should be able to move throughout your potential range easily and comfortably. Adding a light chewing motion will help keep your jaw and throat area relaxed. This is great for those times when you want to work on expanding your range and smoothing out your passagio without making a scene. (Caution: I have been gently kicked under the table in a restaurant more than once when Carole heard me "lightly warming up" a bit too loudly!)

- On this exercise, you will again use the "mah," "bah," and "pah" syllables. Instead of choosing random notes, however, use the following pattern. Once you learn the pattern, move up and down by half steps, keeping the exercise challenging but safe. Always remember the four areas to watch: correct posture, proper breathing, a relaxed throat, and the forward position of your tongue.

- Using the pattern from the preceding exercise, now alternate between the "mah," bah," or "pah" and the "lip buzz" or "bubble."

  The lip buzz is much like the sound babies make when they exhale through vibrating lips—usually accompanied by some saliva! Toddlers refine that sound when they imitate motor or engine noise when playing with cars, trucks, or motorcycles. If you do this same thing through relaxed, loosely vibrating lips, with good posture, and with plenty of breath, you'll find that it's a very, very effective vocal exercise.

First, pretend that you are a small baby blowing bubbles just for fun. Now become a toddler playing with a toy motorcycle and make the appropriate engine noise. Next, imitate a horse by making that same sound through huge, floppy lips. (Feel free to add a shaking head if you're in the mood!) Finally, imagine that you're in Minnesota in the winter. It's -20°, and you've just come into the house after a good game of hockey in the back yard. When your body hits that warm air, you lift your shoulders, shake your head, and bubble. Do that several times.

Now add a sustained melody to the buzzing lips and sing some scales using only the bubble. If your bubbles aren't bubbling, place your index fingers on your cheeks just behind your mouth and push gently. Doing this will relieve tension around your mouth and allow a more desirable, loose, floppy action in your lips.

Once you're comfortably bubbling, go back to the pattern you just learned and alternate between the bubble and "mah," "bah," or "pah." You will immediately notice how relaxed your throat remains while you are using the bubble. You'll also notice that, if your throat gets tense, the bubble stops. This built-in monitor is one of the great features of this exercise. You can only do it while your throat is quite free and relaxed.

• This exercise will help you relax your throat and continue to build that essential bridge between your head and chest registers. I call this exercise the "descending yawn–sigh." Start this two-octave descending exercise with a full, low breath. Simply yawn and then sigh, beginning high in your head and moving down the scale. (Sometimes it helps to start with a light *h*.)

Keep your hand gently massaging your throat as you sing through these exercises. As long as your throat is loose and relaxed, you're doing fine. When your muscles get tight, you need to stop and check your posture, breathing, and articulation. If all is well in these areas and your throat is still tight, then you are probably out of your comfortable range. As you continue to work on these exercises using good technique, your comfortable range will increase.

The Pathway to Expanding Your Range

Your range may not increase as quickly as you like or as significantly as you hope, but you won't know until you try. And disciplined, careful work may even pay off beyond your expectations. As you work through the exercises I've provided, know where you are—your limitations today—so that you'll be able to protect your voice and note your progress. Following the principles for posture, breathing, throat, and tongue and doing some of these exercises daily will keep you moving toward realizing your vocal potential.

A Brief Intermission

❦ Define *vocal range* and the difference between hitting and singing notes. What naturally limits a person's range? What are some of the benefits of expanding your current range?

❦ What is your current range? High note:__ Low note:__ When was your range different? What was it and why do you think it has changed?

❦ Define a singer's comfortable range. What is your comfortable octave?

❦ What was the major point in the discussion of voice classifications? What warning does this section offer to choir leaders? What does the distinction between "God made" and "man defined" mean to you?

❦ What four guidelines for working through these exercises are important principles to follow whenever you sing?

❦ *Maybe it's time to expand your range when it comes to reading Scripture. Perhaps you would define your current range as a few favorite psalms, the Gospels, and some familiar passages from Paul's letters. But what about the Old Testament prophets, the Genesis and Exodus account of the people of Israel, the not-so-easy books of Hebrews and Romans, and the imagery of Revelation? This week choose three passages outside of your biblical comfort zone and ask God to speak to you through them. I bet you'll be surprised by what you learn!*

Note: The audiotapes *Expanding Your Range* and *Tone I* from Star Song's Vocal Fitness Center can help you work on topics discussed in this chapter.

Chapter 6

Planning Your Performance

Think back to the most recent vocal performance you attended. What do you remember now? The music? The performer? The musical accompaniment? The program's overall message? The audience's reaction? How the performance affected you? The technical presentation? A vocal performance is a multifaceted event that can touch people in a variety of ways. And in all vocal performances, a singer or group of singers is involved in the complex process of sharing a message in song.

The broad category we are dealing with here is communications. There is a message (something to be communicated); a transmitter (that's you using your voice to move the airwaves and your facial expressions and physical movement to underscore your message); and a receiver (the listener's ears, eyes, heart, and mind). Since your voice is the instrument being used in this communication process, let's start there.

Your voice needs to be capable of clearly and accurately singing the message you choose to communicate. Your breathing, tone, and diction must be operational. Your knowledge of proper posture and your regular practice of correct breathing will give you confidence in your voice. Your hours of rehearsal add to your sense that you are ready to minister through music.

Choosing Your Songs

But what are you going to sing? How do you choose the songs? Do you believe their messages? Can you relate to the lyrics? What key will you sing the songs in? Do you even know your comfortable range? How's your microphone technique? And in what order will you sing your songs? Proper preparation prevents poor performance, and preparation is what this book is all about. So let's slow down and look at how to select the music for your performance.

If you are considering singing your own compositions, be sure to ask yourself these two questions: "Are these songs the best ones available to communicate my message? Am I more interested in highlighting my own material than I am in the overall impact of my time with my listeners?" If you really want to do your program planning right, ask several qualified people their opinion of your music. If some of your songs pass these tests, use them. If not, don't. They would water down your message.

Are these songs the best ones available to communicate my message? Am I more interested in highlighting my own material than I am in the overall impact of my time with my listeners?

Whether you use original material or songs written by others, choosing a song is one of the most critical elements of your performance. You must be able to honestly relate to the message, or your presentation won't be believable. "But," you may ask, "what about when you study voice in college and sing all kinds of assigned songs? And what about opera stars or Broadway singers who sing whatever role is assigned to them? They're acting and singing, so why can't I?"

The answer is that you can act, and that's a wonderful way to learn voice technique and flexibility. I still love to sing the classical repertoire that I first studied years ago.

The musical and vocal disciplines are unbeatable. But when I am ministering to people through a song with the hope of changing hearts, it's not an act. That kind of music ministry is genuinely from my heart, and the message grows out of my own experience with the Lord. And that's the kind of singing I'm talking about here. I'm not talking about playing a role and pretending to be someone you're not. I'm talking about sharing from the depths of your soul. In light of that, you must be able to relate to your songs. That factor is important to the overall credibility of your performance as well as to the integrity of your ministry.

Recognizing Appropriate Songs

As you consider different songs, keep in mind the following points:

- **Your age**—I've heard 15-year-olds singing testimony songs about their multiple marriages, their suffering children, and the house and car they lost due to their sinful lives. Well, that's just plain foolish. The song's message is not consistent with the singer. I've also heard adults sing about topics they couldn't possibly relate to. It's imperative in ministry that you only sing those messages which you can honestly sing.

- **Your musical background, taste, and style**—A truly great singer and musician can sing almost any style and do it well, but most singers can't. If you are a conservative, 40-year-old who was brought up in the church and never listened to rock-and-roll, don't sing a rock-and-roll song in an effort to relate to the youth of your church. Your performance will probably look and sound like what it is—phony. And, if you're going to sing the music of another culture, make sure your accent and diction are authentic.

You need to know yourself and you need to get to know the music you are considering for your performance. If the songs don't fit, don't sing them. There are plenty of wonderful songs out there, songs that will enable you to communicate the message you want to share in a way that is genuinely you. Don't compromise on this point, or you'll be compromising the effectiveness of your ministry.

Selecting the Key

Now that you've chosen your songs, what key are you going to sing in? I've heard people say, "I like to sing in the key of C." That statement reveals a real lack of knowledge. You see, the key of the song and the range of its notes are completely unrelated. A song can be in the key of C and be low, medium, or high in range.

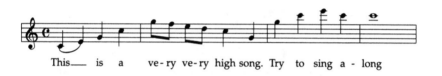

This— is a ve-ry ve-ry high song. Try to sing a - long

This   is   me - di - um and   not   ve - ry   chal - leng - ing.

This   is   get - ting   ve - ry   ve - ry low.

These three examples are all in C, but some would work, some would not. Ask yourself these three questions about each song you've selected:

What is the lowest note?
What is the highest note?
What is the tessitura, or average note?
(Look back at Chapter 5.)

It's important that you know what your comfortable range is so you'll know whether you and a song are a good match. (As a bass, I know that it's one thing for me to sing an occasional high E in a song. It's quite another for me to be spending the entire song on D and E above middle C!)

If you're not a musician, find someone who plays an instrument help you determine your range. Choose a simple chorus, hymn, or song and have that person play it in a number of keys. Note how comfortable the low, high, and average notes are. When you find your comfortable top note, bottom note, and tessitura, write down the results. And remember that we don't all fit perfectly into the category of soprano, alto, tenor, or bass. You might really be in between. Remember, too, that singing in your comfortable range will make a real difference in the quality of your performance.

Let me assure you that there is nothing wrong with transposing a keyboard arrangement into the perfect key for you. If the soundtrack you have is simply not in a comfortable key, don't use it. Look for one that fits you. Don't force your voice to conform to someone else's key. If you are a serious singer, you might even consider having some custom accompaniment tracks made. It can be relatively inexpensive and make all the difference in your performance.

Tips for Using Tracks

Speaking of commercial accompaniment tracks, these tools can be a blessing or a curse. To ensure that they help you improve your singing, follow these tips from RaMarie Swart's article "Staying on the Right 'Track'" (from *The Vocal Coach Newsletter*, Nashville, Star Song Communications, November/December 1990):

1. Choose songs based on content, range, and tessitura suited to your abilities. If you want to stretch your

technique, try something that is challenging but doesn't cause discomfort. If it's uncomfortable for you, it's probably uncomfortable for the listener as well.

2. Learn the song before using the tape. Play it on an instrument using the lead sheet on the J-card that comes with the tape. Or buy and play the full printed score. If you can't read music, motivate yourself to learn. Seek help from your choir director or a friend. To build your confidence and expand your knowledge, take voice or instrument lessons.

3. Don't aggravate your vocal flaws by repeatedly singing with the vocal demo. As the Vocal Coach always says, "Practice makes permanent, but not necessarily perfect."

4. Develop your own interpretation of a new song. Make it your song by using your own creativity and strengths.

5. Vary the songs that you learn so that you perform material that has been recorded by a number of artists. Even better, sing some generic songs that are not identified with anyone in particular.

6. Do not play tapes at high volume. Use them only as background support.

7. While learning a new song, practice a cappella as much as you practice with the tape so that you are able to concentrate on the physical feeling and sound of your voice. Get intimately acquainted with your vocal instrument.

8. Learn and perform some songs without tracks. This will teach you how to work with an accompanist. You may experience initial difficulties, but perseverance will reward you with a surge in your musical proficiency. (You might even perform something unaccompanied if you are musically able to remain accurate.)

Ms. Swart concludes with the important reminder that "God has given you personalized talents to develop. Don't allow this special aspect to be diminished by singing in someone else's shadow. Be inspired by your favorite artists, but don't be a clone!" I agree wholeheartedly!

A Checklist for Planning a Performance

As you prepare for your performance and as you perform, it's important to keep in mind these important questions: "What am I doing?" and "Who am I doing this for?" The following nine questions offer further guidance for your preparation.

1. Who is your audience? The youth of the church? Older people? A general mix? Answering this question will help you answer some of the next questions.
2. What is your message? Never just sing songs for a short period of time. People in the audience can hear that on the radio. Instead, plan your program around whatever goal you want to achieve, and write out that goal. This written statement will help keep you focused. Besides, if you don't have a specific goal, how will you know if you accomplish it?
3. What songs in your repertoire contribute to that message? If necessary, add songs that will help you share your message more effectively.
4. What is the total time available and how will you use that time effectively? Check with the church leadership and conform to the time constraints they give.

   Be sure you have the time mapped out, including time for introductions, announcements, messages, the offering, and so on. Contrary to popular opinion, the Holy Spirit is quite capable of working within a fixed period of time! He is also very good at planning ahead; He isn't limited to spontaneous inspiration and change. Let Him help you plan the concert ahead of time. That way you won't have to plead with Him during the event.

5. How will you open your performance? With talking? With a song that includes audience participation? With something big or something soft? What will be most appropriate for this group of listeners? Don't get locked into a rut. Be fresh and creative. And be sure to address specifically and appropriately each new performance situation.

6. What kind of transitions will you use between songs? If you're going to teach, have the lessons well rehearsed and the Scripture references memorized. (If you are weak here, ask your pastor for assistance.) If your testimony will serve as a transition, make it short and sweet. Don't drag out over ten minutes what can be said in two.

   Use key phrases from previous and upcoming songs. Keep the elements of your program connected. If no transition is needed between several songs, leave it alone. Let the songs speak for themselves. As you can see, there are many ways to handle the transition between songs. Get ideas from watching others and then adapt them to fit who you are.

7. What is your mix of accompaniment—tracks, live piano or guitar, or even a cappella? An all-tracks concert can be wonderful, but if you play an instrument, learn several songs well and use them. This can provide welcome variety, but only if you're proficient on the instrument you choose. The first choices are usually keyboard and guitar, but an instrumental interlude on a trumpet, sax, or flute can be nice, too.

8. In what order will you sing your songs? As you order your songs, be sure there is logical sequence as well as musical variety. Put together a tentative list and then actually sing through it. You will be your

own best critic. When you are happy, run your program by several other people. Because the sequence and pacing of your songs is crucial, you should assemble your program thoughtfully and carefully.

9. How will you close your time? Will you or someone else close with an altar call? Will the program end with an offering, or would that disrupt the mood? Whatever you decide to do, it's important to come to some sort of conclusion. Don't just stop singing.

By the time you've finished, the audience or congregation should have come to a deeper understanding of the Lord and some new decisions about their life. Whenever possible, give them specific time to think through what God is saying to them through your message and encourage them to apply that lesson to their lives. This time of reflection should be part of your program time, not something you expect the audience to do later. They probably won't.

As the Spirit Leads

As I said earlier in the chapter, proper preparation prevents poor performance. And as you have seen, preparing for a vocal performance is not a simple task. You must know what it is you want to communicate and then choose songs that help you share that message. Next, learning the songs—the message, the words, the vowel sounds, the consonant sounds, the rhythms, the melody—so that you have them down cold is no small undertaking. You must also consider your audience, the time factor, the order of your songs, and the kind of transition between songs you want to use. It sounds like a big job and it is a big job, but you don't have to do it alone. Let the Spirit lead as you plan a vocal performance. Count on Him to guide your thoughts, inspire your singing, and help your performance touch hearts and glorify your Lord.

A Brief Intermission

🐛 Why is it important that you relate to the songs you share in your music ministry? Choose five songs (worship choruses, traditional hymns, and contemporary Christian songs) that you easily and genuinely relate to.

🐛 What is your comfortable range? (Go through the exercise in Chapter 5 to determine your range if you don't already know it.) What keys put the songs you listed above in your range?

🐛 In your opinion, what are the advantages and disadvantages of using vocal tracks? When have you or would you use them? When wouldn't you use them?

🐛 Evaluate to the following in someone else's performance:

- Note the order of the songs. Did all the fast or loud songs come together? Or were softer, slower songs interspersed? How effective was this pacing? How logically did the songs flow together?

- What was the singer's main message? How well did the songs work together to communicate that message? Were all the songs appropriate to the singer?

- What musical accompaniment did the performer have? When did he or she use tracks? How effective were the tracks?

- What verbal bridges did the singer use? Did the bridges work? Were any too long or too short?

- How did the concert begin and end?

- What, if anything, did the singer do that you want to avoid doing when you perform? What did you see that you would like to incorporate into your program?

🐛 Look again at the five song titles you listed at the beginning of this intermission and at the nine-point checklist for planning a performance. Now spend some time planning a performance. Choose your own audience and tailor your performance to them. Clearly state your goal and your message. Then select your songs. You may need to add or subtract from your list of five so that you have a consistent message and unified program. Perhaps one of the titles you listed would be the cornerstone of your performance.

Plan a 20- or 30-minute program, your transitions, your accompaniment, and your closing. You might even perform for the video camera, a mirror, or a group of friends. It would be great practice!

🍂 *At some point, it may be appropriate to share your testimony. Right now, in a quiet time with the Lord think through your life with Him. How did you come to know Him? What are some of the most precious lessons He has taught you through the years? What are three or four verses that could help you tell your story? Make this time of reflection a time of praise and thanksgiving.*

Note: The *Performance* audiotape from Star Song's Vocal Fitness Center reinforces some of the important concepts discussed in this chapter.

Chapter 7

Taking Care of Performance Details

In the preceding chapter, you concentrated on choosing songs, an important part of planning your performance. But getting to know the meaning, the story, the sounds, the rhythm, and the melody of your songs is not the only factor that contributes to communicating their message effectively. Your delivery is also important. So now that you've learned the song, it's time to decide how to present or deliver it. Let me suggest that you deliver it clearly, comfortably, and honestly.

- **Clearly**—Anything that comes between your heart and the listener's ear will diminish the message and decrease the effectiveness of your performance. The auditory and visual stimulations that your audience receive are the only means they have to determine what is in your heart, so you want to be sure that

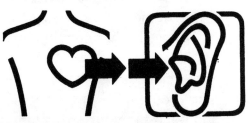

Anything that comes between your heart and the listener's ear will diminish the message and decrease the effectiveness of your performance.

your delivery is clear and sharp. Start by checking your vocal sound and diction with an audiocassette or videocassette recording. If your voice sounds strained or your words are mumbled or unclear, correct the situation. Whatever distracts you may also distract your listeners. I also encourage you to get a second opinion. Share your recording with someone who is qualified and from whom you are willing to receive criticism.

- **Comfortably**—There's no automatic way to achieve a comfortable delivery. Comfort is a quality you have to grow into. But even during the growing, you can increase your comfort quotient by being as physically, mentally, and spiritually prepared as possible. If there is little doubt in your mind about what is going to happen, you will be comfortable, and your ease will put the listener at ease and in a better frame of mind to receive the message you're sharing.

- **Honestly**—Your audience should be able to see that you are being genuine and honest when you perform. We live in an age of hype and con. I disregard many advertising claims I hear because I know that people will say anything they can legally get away with. The folks writing the ad copy are ultimately concerned with their bottom line, not with bettering my life. We Christian ministers and performers must be careful not to fall into that same mold. Are we genuinely concerned about our audience? Are we honestly sharing with them who we are?

The Camera Knows

Once you feel that you're ready to be clear, comfortable, and honest in your presentation, it's time to get in front of the camera or, at the very least, a mirror. By far the most effective tool is a video camera, which you can use to tape yourself in rehearsal. There is no more powerful—and sometimes discouraging—tool. Its neutral, unbiased feedback is brutal, without mercy, and, oh, so valuable. Even if you are just using a mirror, begin to look for the following:

- **Posture**—Your posture speaks to your audience before you do. Is your posture broken and crooked? Is it arrogant and intimidating? Or are you standing in an upright, balanced, and natural position? You need to be. Otherwise, you posture could detract from your message. Do you look comfortable and secure? If not, why not? Know that if you're not comfortable, your audience won't be either.

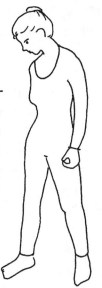

- **Breathing**—Are you breathing with your abdomen, sides, and back rather than heaving your chest? Be sure that your breathing will not be a distraction or limit your vocal quality.
- **Facial expression**—What does your face look like as you sing? Do you look bored? Do you look phony? Is your expression consistent with your message?

Is your posture broken and crooked?

Are you standing in an upright, balanced, and natural position?

Does it visually add to the message? Is it neutral, adding nothing to your performance? Or, worse, is it a distraction? Does your face show so much pain, discomfort, struggle, or fear that the message of the song will never get through? Be honest with yourself as you consider these questions, but don't be discouraged. Ninety-nine percent of us have to work at looking relaxed and having a facial expression that is consistent with our message. It just takes practice.

Try this exercise alone or with the help of a group. As you stand before the camera or a mirror, practice appropriate facial expressions as well as upright posture and good breathing. Develop a repertoire of facial expressions. Learn to reflect joy and delight, fear and terror, concern and compassion, authority and arrogance, honesty and sincerity. Because facial expressions are physical and practice makes permanent, practicing these and other expressions will give you a storehouse of available expressions. Then you won't feel funny when it's time to use them. Like the singing process itself, facial expressions must be practiced. It's a participation sport. No amount of thinking about it will take the place of just doing it.

- **Body movement**—Closely related to facial expression is body movement. Here, though, different guidelines will apply depending on where you are performing or ministering. In settings like a morning worship service in a very traditional church, a facial expression is as far as you can go to physically support the message you are singing. In other settings, you can get away with back flips in the middle of a song. As a rule, however, most singers need to let their bodies—especially their face and arms—be more genuinely involved in the song. There is, for instance, something distracting and almost dishonest about singing of the joy of the Lord while you're standing as if you're in a body cast. If you're going to be no more than a speaker cabinet in clothes, you might just as well play a tape.

  To discover body movements appropriate to the song, practice the song in the following way. First imagine that you're in front of a large crowd without a microphone and if you don't use your face and hands the audience won't get the message. During this practice time, exaggerate what you're saying with your body. You can always tone it down later. Now perform in front of an imaginary group of children. What movements will make your message real to them?

Whenever you perform, find a range and a set of movements that you're comfortable with and don't be afraid to use them. The criticism of being overly expressive is seldom heard.

P.A. Systems: Friend or Foe?

No matter how much you plan and how carefully you work on your delivery, you can be sure that unexpected things will happen when it's time to perform. You'll be better able to deal with life's surprises, though, when you've thought about possible challenges and disasters beforehand. That's what we're going to do now.

When you perform, you'll probably be working with a P.A. system and a sound engineer. Most churches these days have some sort of sound reinforcement system, but they vary greatly in quality and effectiveness. Some churches will have 50-year-old single speaker systems with an on–off switch and a preset volume—and that's it in the way of controls. Some have $100,000 systems that come with special effects capabilities, monitors, and highly trained sound engineers. But most sound systems you'll encounter will fall in between these extremes, so that's what I'll talk about here.

- *Microphones* can be a real blessing if they're used correctly, and here are some tips. Because part of your communication is visual, don't cover your mouth with the microphone. Hold the microphone just below your mouth in front of your chin and about three or four inches in front of you. Keep that position unless you are

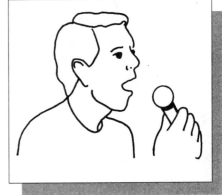

Hold the microphone just below your mouth in front of your chin and about three or four inches in front of you.

singing either extremely loudly (for that, you may move the mike a bit farther away) or very, very softly (then move the mike a bit closer to give more presence).

- It's a great mistake to assume that, just because you are experienced and the sound person is experienced, all will run smoothly. Too many things can go wrong. So to make sure that you and the person running the sound are both comfortable with what is going to happen during your performance, be sure to schedule a *sound check*. This should be a relaxed time after you have warmed up your voice (otherwise the real you won't be coming out) and well in advance of the service or concert (maybe even the night before).

  In about 10 or 15 minutes, you and the engineer can get to know each other. During that time, be sure to sing a sample of your loudest and softest singing so there are no surprises. If you don't offer this preview, the engineer may not realize that you are changing volume and intensity on purpose and may start trying to compensate for the changes.

- Establish *signals* with the sound person in case things get out of balance. Here are some standard signals that communicate to the sound person what you are hearing on the platform or stage, not necessarily what is going on in the house:

  1. If you need to hear more of your voice, point to the mike and then up. Point to the mike and then down if your voice is too loud.
  2. If you need to adjust the track or accompaniment level, spin your index finger like a spinning tape and then point up or down.
  3. If you can't hear, either point to the monitor speaker and up or to your ear.

  If your signals don't get through and things get sticky during your performance, I suggest just talking politely to the sound person on the mike. It's better to have things disrupted briefly than to play it cool and ruin the whole event.

- Besides reviewing hand signals, be sure to supply your sound person with *written information.* First, give him or her a list of your songs in the order you propose to sing them. If your performance starts to run long or you feel you need to change, you can simply ask for that change. You might also, in advance, provide some optional orders and very clear lead-ins as cues. (Those lead-ins might include the subject or even the title of the song.) You should also write down what you expect to be saying right before you want the tape to start running. A nod of the head can help the sound person stay with you. These kinds of written and physical cues are the least you can do to help someone who is not familiar with you and your concert help you as you perform!

Since there are numerous ways to handle these signals or cues, only a sound check will prevent misunderstandings. If you employ your own sound person, of course you don't have to worry about such an extensive sound check. For most of us, however, a thorough sound check makes all the difference in our concerts. During my pre-performance sound checks as well as my concerts, my wife, Carole, stands with the sound person and alerts him or her to what is going on. She doesn't have to run the board, and the sound person doesn't have to try to guess at what I'll do next. Having Carole there gives me the best of both worlds: I don't have to pay for a personal engineer, but I still have someone at the board who knows my music and ministry well.

Some More Brass Tacks

We're not quite at the end of our list. Here are some other practical considerations before you start performing.

• How will you *dress*? It is critical that what you wear is appropriate to the event and complements both you and the situation. If your clothing is too tight, too wild, or ill-fitting, it will detract from your ministry. While you certainly don't have to go out and spend major dollars on new outfits, you must remember that the visual you is part of the message you are communicating. Notice, too, what distracts you about the appearance of other performers, and learn from them what to avoid when you're on stage.

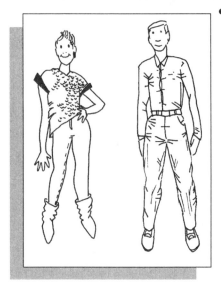

If your clothing is too tight, too wild, or ill-fitting, it will detract from your ministry.

• Have you scheduled some serious *rest* time before the event? It takes more energy than most people realize to minister effectively and powerfully from the platform. If you aren't physically rested, you may not have all you need to be your best. So don't be shy about proclaiming to your friends and family that you are going to pace yourself and rest before any scheduled performance. If you are flying to your concert destination, you need to be even more careful. The dehydration and fatigue caused by air travel can be substantial, and you must allow recovery time.

• Another very important issue is proper *nutrition*. You can be as inspired as you want, but if you have been living on fast food and diet soda, your body is in no condition to minister effectively. Your voice is not some mysterious or magical instrument. It is physical, and that means everything you do to your body

affects your voice. And healthy
eating will mean a stronger body
and a stronger voice.

Are you living on fast food and diet soda? Your body will be in no condition to minister effectively.

- Finally, it's crucial that you
appropri-ate the necessary time
before your sound check for an
adequate *warm-up*. For a thorough warm-up, get alone in a
quiet room. Prepare your mind
and spirit and stretch out your
body. Take time to align your
posture, and then begin some
vocal exercises. Start slowly with
yawns and sighs, progressing to
scales sung with different syllables (you want to wake up
your tongue, teeth, and lips) and
ending with a song that you'll

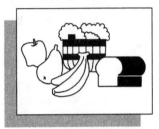

Healthy eating will mean a stronger body and a stronger voice.

be performing. First sing the words at a single pitch
and check to see that your posture, breathing, and
diction are all working together. Then sing the song
fully, but don't wear yourself out. It's also a good
idea to run through any spoken comments you plan
to make.

Proper Preparation . . .

Vocal performance. It's the process of using your voice to
communicate a message that will impact the lives of others. You need to prepare the physical with proper vocal
training, diet, and rest; the mind and emotions with a clear
understanding of your calling and clearly defined goals
for your ministry; and the spirit by prayerfully letting the
Holy Spirit guide you each step of the way. If you prayerfully and responsibly consider each area we've discussed
in this chapter and the previous one, and actively work to
improve, you will be a better performer. After all, proper

preparation prevents poor performance. By using your time and resources well, you can do a better job as a kingdom communicator.

A Brief Intermission

- ❦ What three qualities should characterize your delivery? Why is each of these important? And how can you develop them?
- ❦ Choose two favorite songs, one upbeat and the other more reverent. Now work on developing appropriate facial expressions and body movements. Have one set of expressions and movements for a Sunday morning worship service and another for the high-school youth group meeting. Be sure your facial expressions and physical movements are logical and consistent with your songs.
- ❦ Look again at the program you planned in Chapter 6. Now plan a sound check that would help you and your sound engineer prepare for your concert. Also write out the information about your program (order of song, lead-ins, options, etc.) that the engineer would need to do his or her job well.
- ❦ How can dress enhance or detract from a vocal performance? What factors influence your choice of what to wear when you perform?
- ❦ Describe your typical preperformance warm-up. Then rate its effectiveness ("1" is "Do I have to go out now?" and "10" is "I'm ready!!"). What can you do to improve your warm-up?
- ❦ *What does God's Word teach about not being a stumbling block? Read and meditate on the following passages:*
    Romans 14:13-23
    1 Corinthians 8:9-13
    2 Corinthians 6:3
    1 John 3:10-11

Let the Scripture be a mirror. What do these teachings say to you about the plans you make for your vocal performances? Do you need to adjust any attitudes or change your approach to planning a concert?

At Star Song's Vocal Fitness Center, you'll find the following tools for working on topics discussed in this chapter: *The Vocal Workout* book, *The Vocal Aerobic Video*, and the audiotapes *Breathing I & II, Daily Workout for Hi Voice I, II & III,* and *Daily Workout for Lo Voice I, II, & III.*

Chapter 8

Checking Your Heart: The Why of It All

Life has undoubtedly taught you that the best-laid plans can fall apart due to unforeseen circumstances. But even the most carefully planned concert—one that is completely free of hitches—will fall flat if you, the performer, are not properly motivated. Your heart can be the life or death of your music ministry.

Through the years, I've seen people with inspiration and aspiration who have spent no time on preparation, and they shouldn't be ministering from the platform. I've also seen folks who have a lot of training but no proper spiritual inspiration, and they definitely shouldn't be ministering either. Those people who should be ministering are those who have found a balance between inspiration and preparation. How do you know if you have it? How do you know if you're ready to minister?

"Your heart can be life or death in your music ministry"

First, you need to honestly check your heart. What are your motives? Why do you want to minister? Is God calling you to minister? Once you feel you're ready, you need to take the difficult step of allowing those people in leadership over you to give their approval and blessing—and I'm not referring to your family and friends. You need to have the approval of people who can, with spiritual and technical objectivity, evaluate what you are doing. Remember that it's inspiration plus preparation that makes the minister.

Inspired? Prepared? Or Both?

As I wrote in Chapter 1—and it's so important that it bears repeating here—a music ministry requires much more than an emotional, sentimental, or even spiritual pull. A ministry that will bear fruit for God's kingdom requires from the person ministering a thoroughly thought-out commitment, adequate vocal and spiritual preparation, unshakable integrity, a praying support team, a regular prayer life, and constant communication with the Lord and with close friends who can hold you accountable to your work.

- Consider the young singer who thinks singing is fun. Being a star with albums, audiences, buses, and big bucks sounds great. The motivation here is the apparent glamour and excitement of it all. This singer will be in a hurry to sound good, sing high, and mimic the artists who are making it big. A slow, step-by-step, multi-year program of preparation and ongoing discipline will not sound especially exciting to him or her. But replacing proper boot camp with clever marketing just won't make a ministry effective.
- Now consider the singer, young or old, who was born with an exceptional voice. He has sung since childhood, always receiving great praise and commendation. This person has never thought about seriously studying voice. Why should he? His voice has always worked—and has always worked well. Consequently, he may never have the drive or discipline to make his voice the best it can be. In time, his voice—the musical instrument God created and

entrusted to him—will begin to tire and fail, and that can happen prematurely whenever singers don't learn how to care for their voice.

- Then there are the positively driven "I-just-have-to-sing" singers. It feels good. It's right. They just know it, and nothing can change that. They are gifted and equipped and willing to do whatever it takes to sing better. They are literally inspired to sing even if there is no audience or acclaim because singing is who they are. This is a good place to be, and it makes for a teachable student and a healthy position from which to minister.

- There's also the message-driven singer. Folks in this category are convinced from the tip of their toes to the top of their head that they have a life-changing, world-changing message, one that was birthed in their spirit and simply has to get out. And out it will come, with or without skill. If these singers with a message can sit still long enough to study, the combination of inspiration and preparation is unbeatable. If they can't, the message will mature, but the instrument that delivers it will wear out. It simply won't be there for the long run.

Where are you? Any of the above categories—and still others—are acceptable. There are no wrong answers. But you do need to identify and acknowledge where you are right now in terms of inspiration and preparation. You may also want to make some serious adjustments in how you think about the area of your voice and the possibility of using it in a music ministry. After all, if you don't like what's going on in any area of your life, the best way to change it is from the inside out.

Another Hard Question

One way to determine the "why of it all" behind your interest in a music ministry is to spend time honestly thinking about the following questions: Are you striving primarily for AIRplay or HEARTplay? Which is the most important to you?

First of all, know that one does not necessarily follow the other. Some of the finest songs ever written will never reach the charts because they aren't presented at the right place at the right time. The same goes for singers. If singers aren't marketable in a given social climate, they will never sign a major recording contract. That fact, however, has little to do with the legitimacy or effectiveness of their ministry. Nowhere does the Bible state that a recording contract or nationwide airplay is to be the goal or measure of the Christian musician. The goal is to minister life, freedom, and transformation to the world at whatever level and in whatever situation you may find yourself.

Where Is Your Heart?

If you wanted to minister at the Church of the Coastland in Huntington Beach, California, Pastor Steve Purdue would ask you the following questions, and these questions may help you determine whether you are ready to minister for the Lord:

1. Are your gifts, talents, and abilities in the control of the Lord Jesus Christ?
2. Have they been adequately refined and polished in your own local church setting?
3. Are you responding to the call of the Holy Spirit and being sent out by Him to the church at large as confirmed by your pastors and elders?
4. Are you coming to our congregation to serve and fit in to what the Holy Spirit is doing here?
5. Will you submit to the pastor and elders of the congregation you are ministering to—even when you think they are wrong?
6. Will you be willing to serve, fit in, and minister

wherever the Holy Spirit sends you, even if there isn't financial remuneration?

These questions may be difficult to answer, but they may also help you determine where your heart is.

"To Whom Much Is Given . . ."

Jesus said, "Everyone to whom much is given, of him will much be required" (Luke 12:48), and the demands of the music ministry can bring into sharp focus the truth of this teaching. The more talented you are, the greater the temptation to minister for airplay rather than heartplay. In fact, the more talented you are, the more integrity you need in order to survive the temptations the world offers. At the beginning, your intentions may be pure and your love for the Lord strong, but a weak character or a ministry undertaken without proper accountability and prayer support can mean failure of your ministry and, even more importantly, the breakdown of your relationship with Jesus.

Let me remind you again that the only way to be a functioning Christian is to have a relationship with the Lord Jesus Christ, to have recognized Him as the Son of God, and to be walking with Him as Lord of your life. Don't be misled—you can't skip that last step.

At the same time, the only way to become a musician is to know something about music. True, you can learn much through trial and error, and many singers and musicians do so. But that kind of haphazard effort rarely accomplishes what disciplined study with a qualified vocal coach or music teacher can. As a result, music ministers who really learn to use music well are few and far between. In fact, more and more, we are seeing that today's successful and most popular performers—in every musical style— are studied, trained singers. We're right back to where we were earlier in this chapter: it's inspiration plus preparation that makes the music minister.

One Last Word

So what is God calling you to do for this season? Is this a time to plant, to gain vocal skills and spiritual strength, or is this a time to reap the skills that you've long been sowing? Is this a time for you to keep silent and prepare for ministry, or is this a time for you to speak out for the Lord?

I encourage you to move carefully, listening closely for God's guidance each step of the way. Being a self-taught ministry burnout may give you a dramatic testimony, but God would rather have you be a flame for His kingdom for a long time. A person who has submitted to the molding of the Potter's hands, who has walked consistently with Jesus and learned much along the way, who has come to see people through the loving and compassionate eyes of the Father—this kind of person offers a ministry that is much more valuable to the work of the Lord than the flame that burned brightly but all too briefly.

Praise God for the gift of your voice! Praise God for a heart that wants to serve Him! And praise Him that He always hears and responds to His child who cries, "Here am I! Send me!" (Isa. 6:8). May God bless you with a rich and fruitful ministry for Him.

A Brief Intermission

- "Your heart can be the life or death of your music ministry." What part of this chapter offered you the clearest insight into your heart? What did you learn?
- Inspiration and preparation (and that includes being musically prepared as well as having a group supporting you with prayer and holding you accountable to the spiritual integrity of your ministry) are fundamental to a strong and effective ministry. Evaluate yourself on those counts: What/who has served or is serving as inspiration in your life? What message(s) do you feel inspired to share? With whom do you feel called to share? What have you

done and what are you doing to prepare yourself vocally and musically for ministry? What are you doing to be prepared spiritually? Who will be holding you accountable to your work for the Lord and praying for that work? What areas of your life need more preparation? What will you do to become better prepared?

🍂 Airplay or heartplay—that phrase captures one of the major battlefields in music ministry today. Why do you want to be involved in a music ministry? What are your goals and dreams? What do you feel God is calling you to do right now? Look at how you answered that question at the end of Chapter 1. What changes, if any, have you made as you've worked through this book? And how does God's call for your life fit with your goals and dreams?

🍂 Life offers us lessons about burnout, even burnout in the ministry. What have you learned by watching other people struggle to serve the Lord with integrity and effectiveness? Don't name names, but do share what you've learned—both good and bad—from people who have gone into music ministry before you. Be sure to include lessons from the positive role models as well as from those who have struggled.

🍂 What season of life do you find yourself in right now? As I asked at the close of the chapter, is this a time to plant, to gain vocal skills and spiritual strength, or is this a time to reap the skills that you've long been sowing? Is this a time for you to keep silent and prepare for ministry, or is this a time for you to speak out for the Lord? Or is this yet a different season for you? Describe the season you're in and be specific about what actions you are taking appropriate to that season.

❧ *This week, spend some time studying the life and ministry of Moses, Paul, Peter, or another biblical figure whose ministry did not follow the desired or expected path. What did that person do when God called? What did that person—and you—learn from his objecting to, fighting, and eventually following or not following that call? Thank God for that lesson as well as for His wisdom, His patience, His forgiveness, and His love.*

Ten Steps to Correct Breathing

If there's one near you, grab a two-year old! Better yet, just watch him or her breathe. You can't find a better model of correct breathing! Notice the posture: head up; shoulders level; ears, shoulders, hips, knees, and ankles in perfect alignment; and a round tummy made quite obvious by the in-and-out movement of deep, full breaths.

We adults offer a less pretty picture of good posture or proper breathing. We are victims of poor role models, laziness, weariness, and all-too-human vanities like constrictive clothing and the compulsion to hold our tummies tucked in unnaturally tight. As a result, our posture and our breathing—and our singing and our speaking—suffer.

But it doesn't have to be that way! Loosen your waistband, relax, and take the following ten easy steps to correct breathing:

1. Start with proper posture. Keeping your shoulders relaxed, lift your hands straight up over your head. Now, with your chin level (parallel to the floor, not tilted up), allow your head to balance naturally between your shoulders. Imagine that a "posture string" is lifting you up from the top of your head. Your ears, shoulders, hips, knees, and ankles should be in perfect alignment. Practice in front of a mirror at first so that you can be sure you're teaching your muscles to memorize the right position.

2. Keeping your chest and ribs stable and still, gradually extend your arms out to your sides until they're

parallel with the floor. You are making a *T* with your body.

3. Without moving your chest and ribs, gently inhale. Allow your lower abdomen (your tummy) to expand and drop away to receive the breath. Your entire waist—front, sides, and back—should be involved.

4. Exhale in small breaths, keeping your chest and ribs comfortably expanded.

Floor Work

5. Lie down on the floor on your back. Get comfortable. Rest your arms loosely at your sides. Feel free to use a small pillow or book for your head. To ease any tension in your back, bend your knees up, keeping your feet flat on the floor. Now relax and again, keeping your chest still, use your abdominal muscles to inhale and exhale. By now you should be very aware of a healthy expansion of the abdominal area all the way from the pelvic bones to the sternum (the base of your breastbone). You'll also notice a significant expansion around the sides of your waist and your back below your ribs and above your hips.

6. As you breathe, place one hand on your abdomen and the other on your collarbone. Your abdomen should be moving, and your collarbone should be still. Let this coordinated rhythm of still chest and expanding/contracting abdomen become part of you. Practice every day.

7. Now, still on your back, extend your arms out into a *T* position and continue to breathe, taking deeper breaths. As you exhale, notice that your abdomen naturally contracts first; then your sides contract. Your back strives to remain expanded to give support.

8. Place your hands behind your head, keeping your elbows on the floor. Keeping your chest still, begin

rhythmically taking in short breaths and blowing out short breaths. Try this several times on a four-count. When you're ready, advance to an eight-count.

Chair Work

9. Now take a seat on a firm chair and lean forward, resting your elbows on your knees. Even thoug you're tilted forward, your head, chest, ribs, and pelvis should be in perfect alignment. Now sip in a slow breath through your mouth. Allow your waist (front, sides, and back) to fully expand. Notice how your chest doesn't even need to help. Instead, you should feel your abdominal, back, and side muscles getting involved. Exhale with a gentle hiss, letting those abdominal muscles do most of the work.

10. Still sitting, let your "posture string" lift your head and chest into an upright sitting position. Again, feel the alignment of your head, chest, ribs, and pelvis. Now repeat the sip/hiss pattern you practiced before: sip in a breath and hiss it out, keeping your chest still and letting your abdominal muscles do the work.

Alternate Steps 9 and 10 several times, letting the relationship between your posture and your breathing muscles become firmly established in your mind and in your muscles. When they are, proper posture and correct breathing will seem natural as you're standing, sitting, speaking, and singing. Remember that muscles have memory and practice makes permanent, so be sure that you're practicing proper posture and correct breathing.

Based on "Ten Steps to Correct Breathing" by Chris Beatty (*The Vocal Coach Newsletter*, Nashville: Star Song Communications, May/June 1990, pp. 1, 6).

Dealing with the Unexpected: Laryngitis and Colds

It's every singer's nightmare come true—laryngitis the day of the concert. It's every speaker's worst-case scenario—a cold the day of the sermon or presentation.

I talked to Dr. Richard W. Quisling, an otolaryngologist in Nashville as well as an experienced vocalist, and Dr. Don C. McLarey, an otolaryngologist and worship leader in Carlsbad, New Mexico, about what to do when germs try to interfere with ministry. Let me share some of their medical wisdom in the hopes that you never have to use it!

Laryngitis

What is laryngitis? We all know it from experience as the frustrating absence of a voice. Physiologically, though, laryngitis is the swelling of the various tissues in the larynx (hence the name). It is caused by a virus, allergies, or vocal abuse (such as cheering for your favorite team), and there is no "safe and instant" cure.

If you get laryngitis and your voice disappears, don't sing, don't talk, and definitely don't whisper. Like a sprained ankle, your laryngitis will heal faster if you don't use the muscles that produce your voice. Furthermore, continuing to use those swollen tissues—just like continuing to walk on a sprained ankle—can lead to serious and permanent damage.

Also, if you get laryngitis, don't treat the problem with drugs. Research has shown that most cases of laryngitis are not responsive to medication. In fact, overzealous use of over-the-counter and prescription drugs can actually hinder your healing. We recommend that you avoid the following:

- Antihistamines, which tend to dry out the respirator tract;
- Inhalants, some of which can be addictive;
- Anesthetic sprays, which mask symptoms and encourage you to use a voice that could be seriously damaged by that use; and
- Aspirin, which some tests suggest may increase the risk of vocal hemorrhage (women are more susceptible to this than men).

So, you're wondering, what can you do when laryngitis strikes? The best thing to do is to moisturize the mucous membranes in your throat. And what's best for that? Water. (Steam is wonderful, as well as Entertainer's Secret—see product informatin in the back of this book) Resign yourself to several days of voicelessness—no singing, no speaking—and moisturize, moisturize, moisturize.

The Common Cold

You probably aren't at all surprised to hear that colds are the most frequent type of infection that people experience. On average, you'll have two to five colds a year. They'll usually last only three or four days, but those days can be uncomfortable. They may also be a time of greater risk for more serious respiratory infections.

When the cold virus first hits, there is usually a dull, burning sensation in the back of the nose and upper part of the throat. Then comes the "runny nose" and "postnasal drip," the aches and pains, and the generally washed-out feeling. As the cold progresses, you may also experience a hacking cough, mild to severe hoarseness, a scratchy throat, a low-grade fever, and plugged ears. If these symptoms intensify or last longer than five days, see a doctor. You don't want to find yourself dealing with bronchitis, sinusitis, or a middle-ear infection.

Unfortunately, there is no known cure for a cold virus. Modern medicine, however, does offer various ways of easing the symptoms. The steam inhaler is probably the most helpful tool available. Decongestants, antihistamines, and over-the-counter nasal sprays can also help ease your discomfort. Even so, nothing can replace plenty of rest and plenty of fluids when it comes to fighting the bug.

Preventive Measures

Preventing laryngitis and colds involves practices which are important for everyday good health.

- Are you drinking enough water during the day? When normal secretion of saliva and mucus is depressed, the vocal lubrication that remains does not adequately hydrate the underlying membranes. Consequently, these membranes are dry and dangerously vulnerable. Laryngitis can result.
- Are you getting enough rest? A tired body is a weakened body, a body more susceptible to germs and viruses and slower to recover when those germs and viruses invade.
- Are you eating healthy, well-balanced meals? Your body needs fuel to function and to fight off diseases.
- Dr. Quisling also advises that singers and speakers taking the following medications avoid demanding vocalization:
  - Sedatives like valium and beta blockers reduce the ability of the voice to make proper muscular actions. You may find yourself less jittery, but you may also have lost the competitive or performance edge when you sing.
  - Diuretics which cause the elimination of excess fluid are not appropriate for singers who need well-lubricated throats.
  - Steroids should only be considered under the

strictest medical supervision. Long-term use can
mean serious side effects and vocal suicide.
- Mucus-thinning medications are not helpful to
  the majority of people. Most of us struggle with
  too little rather than too much or too thick
  lubrication.

Don't hesitate to consult a physician if laryngitis hits
again and again or if you always seem to be battling a
cold. Something else may be going on, and you may be
glad that the laryngitis or cold got you into the doctor's
office for the care you needed. Usually, however, these
common illnesses are signs that we're not taking good care
of ourselves. Be patient when the symptoms strike and be
wise about general health care.

Based on "When You Get Laryngitis . . . " by Richard W. Quisling,
M.D., and Chris Beatty (*The Vocal Coach Newsletter*, Nashville: Star
Song Communications, May/June 1990, p. 5) and "Carols, Chorales,
and Coughs—The Sounds of the Holiday Season" by Don C. McLarey,
M.D. (*The Vocal Coach Newsletter*, Nashville: Star Song Communica-
tions, November/December 1990, p. 5)

The Vocal Coach Product Line

If you have any questions about the Vocal Coach line of products and how they can be applied personally or in a group setting, contact The Upright Foundation, P.O. Box 699, Lindale, TX 75771, or call (903) 882-9602, or fax (903) 882-6534.

Blending 1
Do you have difficulty blending your voice with others? Here is a logical approach to the problem, whether you are part of a small group or a large choir .... **Audiotape, $9.99**

Breathing 1
This foundational tape provides basic exercises for breath control for speakers and singers .... **Audiotape, $9.99**

Breathing 2
An advanced vocal exercise tape, *Breathing 2* gives exercises that will expand and challenge those who sing or speak extensively .... **Audiotape, $9.99**

Daily Workout Hi Voice 1
This daily workout accompanies you through exercises specifically designed for sopranos and tenors at a beginning level of vocal proficiency .... **Audiotape, $9.99**

Daily Workout Hi Voice 2
This daily workout accompanies you through exercises specifically designed for sopranos and tenors at an intermediate level of vocal proficiency .... **Audiotape, $9.99**

Daily Workout Hi Voice 3

This daily workout accompanies you through exercises specifically designed for sopranos and tenors at an advanced level of vocal proficiency.............**Audiotape, $9.99**

Daily Workout Lo Voice 1

This daily workout accompanies you through exercises specifically designed for alto and bass singers at a beginning level of vocal proficiency.................**Audiotape, $9.99**

Daily Workout Lo Voice 2

This daily workout accompanies you through exercises specifically designed for alto and bass singers at an intermediate level of vocal proficiency...........**Audiotape, $9.99**

Daily Workout Lo Voice 3

This daily workout accompanies you through exercises specifically designed for alto and bass singers at an advanced level of vocal proficiency.............**Audiotape, $9.99**

Diction 1

This popular tape provides a practical approach to clear pronunciation. Ideal for both speakers and singers ....**Audiotape, $9.99**

Expanding Your Range

Learn how to expand and increase your vocal ability and become a flexible and dynamic singer. These principles and exercises will lead you through a systematic program to achieve maximum vocal range.............**Audiotape, $9.99**

Performance: How to Learn and Deliver a Song

This entertaining audio tape covers such topics as how to learn a song, choosing music that is suited for your voice, how to personalize a song, and using prerecorded tracks ....**Audiotape, $9.99**

Tone 1
This foundational tape features exercises to help speakers and singers develop a pleasing, resonant vocal sound quality ....**Audiotape, $9.99**

The Vocal Aerobic Workout Video
A program of exercises for the body and the voice, this 40-minute video is the ideal way to tone and maintain the gift that God has given us in our voices........**Videotape, $19.99**

The Vocal Coach Speakers Video Workshop
Perfect for pastors and teachers, *The Vocal Coach Speakers Video* is also designed for anyone who wants to speak with more confidence and poise ....**Videotape, $19.99**

The Vocal Coach Video Workshop
This comprehensive three-hour vocal workshop systematically teaches the viewer how to develop proper breathing, posture, and warm-up techniques for the optimum health and fitness of the voice ....**Two videotapes, $69.99**

The Vocal Workout Video
A digest of key sections from *The Vocal Coach Video Workshop*, this 80-minute tape features Christian performing artists Steve Green, Twila Paris, and Rick Florian..**Videotape, $19.99**

Warm-up 1
This practical tape provides warm-up exercises to prepare your voice for the daily challenges of singing and speaking ....**Audiotape, $9.99**

Warm-up 2
A follow-up to *Warm-up 1*, this advanced training tape is for complex vocal patterns and provides special emphasis on vocal flexibility ....**Audiotape, $9.99**

Intensive Vocal Training Schools by Chris and Carole Beatty

For those who are serious about learning how to use their voices to the fullest we offer Intensive Vocal Training Schools each year in Nashville, Tennessee. These Sunday-through-Thursday schools are limited to 20. Small interactive classes, videotaping, and even time in a recording studio will help you expand your vision and abilities in a safe, noncompetitive setting. For more information write The Upright Foundation, IVTS, Star Song Communications, P.O. Box 150009, Nashville, TN 37215.

Workshops and Concerts

Vocal Fitness workshops and concerts with Chris and Carole Beatty are offered year-round throughout the United States and Canada. The workshops are life changing for singers and speakers; the concerts are challenging and inspirational. For details on workshops and concerts contact The Upright Foundation, P.O. Box 699, Lindale, TX 75771, or call (903) 882-9602.

Entertainer's Secret Throat Spray

Immediately restores vocal quality and improves comfort. Formulated to resemble and supplement the body's own secretions that soothe the vital mucous membranes in the throat and larynx. A topical moisturizer and lubricant for the throat, containing aloe vera gel and glycerin. Contact the Upright Foundation, P.O. Box 699, Lindale, TX 75771, or call (903) 882-9602.

Chris and Carole Beatty: The Vocal Coaches

Vocal teachers. Songwriters. Pastors. Authors. Recording artists. These are just a few of the roles that Chris and Carole Beatty have played in their long and illustrious careers. Better known to the thousands of students they have worked with for over two decades as "The Vocal Coaches," Chris and Carole have been instrumental in developing and preserving the voices of such renowned soloists, speakers, and choral groups as Pat and Debby Boone, Jack Hayford, Steve Green, Twila Paris, Dallas Holm, The 2nd Chapter of Acts, The Continental Singers, and The African Children's Choir.

Chris and Carole's roots in music and the arts are as deep as their commitment to witnessing their Christian faith to everyone they train. Chris is the son of a voice teacher and the nephew of internationally acclaimed composer Samuel Barber *(Adagio for Strings)*. His many years of experience as a singer with The Chicago Symphony Chorus, Lyric Opera, Norman Luboff Choir, Ray Coniff Singers, and on the Kay Starr Show have given him an appreciation and adeptness for the rich tapestry of all forms of vocal stylings. Chris' formal training in voice occurred at Northern Illinois University, the Chicago Musical College of Roosevelt University, and with legendary choral director Margaret Hillis and voice teacher Harvey Ringel. Chris is also a gifted composer who has drafted such now-classic worship hymns as *Holy Ground, Holy Are You, Lord,* and *You Are Worthy*. Carole's background in theatre, staging, and dance has given her keen insight into all levels of performance and presentation. Together their diverse talents and backgrounds have made them indispensible instructors to countless famous, and not-so-famous, vocalists.

Committed to the belief that those who communicate with a clear and strong voice will dramatically effect those around them, Chris and Carole travel ten months each year conducting three- and six-hour Vocal Fitness Workshops and seminars throughout the United States and Canada. In conjunction with their publisher, Star Song Communications, they have developed, written, and produced 19 best-selling audiotapes and videotapes, a bimonthly eponymously titled newsletter, and two instructional books. Each of these products reflects the professional commitment Chris and Carole have made to providing proven, effective, and essential vocal training techniques. Their comprehensive approach to developing the voice is demonstrated in the diversity of their product line and the topics they cover in their workshops—including posture, breathing, phonation, projection, tone, articulation, and blending.

In oral communication—whether through song, sermon, or lecture—it is the quality and presentation of the voice that inspires the listener to action. Developing and maintaining the voice, therefore, is an important responsibility for those who have been called to proclaim the Gospel of Jesus Christ. Chris and Carole Beatty have dedicated their lives to equipping ministers with the tools they need to have their words taken seriously and to ensuring that the good news of salvation be presented in a manner worthy of its message.